HOW TO WIN AT

MTV THE CHALLENGE

AND LIFE

HOW TO WIN AT
MTV THE
CHALLENGE
AND LIFE

A Champion's Guide to Eliminating Obstacles, Winning Friends, and Making That Money

SYDNEY BUCKSBAUM

MTV
Entertainment
BOOKS

NEW YORK   LONDON   TORONTO   SYDNEY   NEW DELHI

An Imprint of Simon & Schuster, Inc.
1230 Avenue of the Americas
New York, NY 10020

First MTV Books/Atria Books hardcover edition October 2022

ATRIA BOOKS and colophon are registered trademarks of Simon & Schuster, Inc.

For information about special discounts for bulk purchases, please contact Simon & Schuster Special Sales at 1-866-506-1949 or business@simonandschuster.com.

The Simon & Schuster Speakers Bureau can bring authors to your live event. For more information or to book an event, contact the Simon & Schuster Speakers Bureau at 1-866-248-3049 or visit our website at www.simonspeakers.com.

Interior design by Kris Tobiassen of Matchbook Digital
Cover key art by LA Associates
Cover design by Raphael A. Geroni-Cithin

Photo credits: courtesy of MTV: pp. 55, 130, 194, 236; courtesy of Landon Lueck: p. 188; courtesy of Cynthia Roberts: p. 10; courtesy of Rachel Robinson: p. 94; Laura Barisonzi for MTV: pp. 6, 32, 64, 90, 140, 152, 159, 183; Jamie Cary for MTV: p. 40; Rene Cervantes for MTV: pp. 50, 137, 162, 167, 206; James Dimmock for MTV: pp. 72, 82, 116, 174; Daymon Gardner for MTV: p. 24; Riccardo Giardina for MTV: p. 230; Jesus Paz for MTV: p. 146; Juan Cruz Rabaglia for MTV: pp. 14, 19, 104, 111, 204; Tyler Richardson for MTV: p. 216; Agustina Russo: p. 226

Manufactured in the United States of America

1 3 5 7 9 10 8 6 4 2

Library of Congress Cataloging-in-Publication Data available at
https://lccn.loc.gov/2022022240.

ISBN 978-1-6680-0874-4
ISBN 978-1-6680-0875-1 (ebook)

CONTENTS

INTRODUCTION

Who is the greatest *Challenge* champion of all time?

Ask any fan of MTV's long-running reality competition series, and you'll always get a different answer. Everyone's got their favorite, and they'll passionately tell you why. For some, it's as easy as looking at the cold, hard facts: Johnny "Bananas" Devenanzio has won seven times, more than any other champ in the history of the show, while Chris "C.T." Tamburello has won the most money, raking in over $1.365 million. For others, it's more about consistency and performance: *Challenge* superhero Landon Lueck's three wins out of four seasons is truly impressive, and hardly anyone has ever beat Alton Williams in a one-on-one matchup. Some fans focus on other stats, like how Darrell Taylor has won the most seasons in a row—a record he set fifteen years ago with his fourth championship that no one has ever been able to break since then.

But what about the other, more subjective ways to judge who is the best? Players who have made history like Veronica Portillo—the first person to win three times—and Cara Maria Sorbello—the first solo winner of *The Challenge*—are legendary. So are competitors who remain undefeated in eliminations, like Emily Schromm, or who continuously slay giants in jaw-dropping displays of power and sheer force of will, like Derrick Kosinski. And what about those who keep themselves out of eliminations by executing a flawless political or social game? That's just as difficult, but achieved by using a completely different set of skills. How are you supposed to compare the puzzle masters to the challenge beasts, the political masterminds to the social butterflies, when they all excel in equally important areas of the game? And is it more impressive to win consistently or to show improvement over the course of someone's *Challenge* career? You can't forget the obvious influence of each season's theme, format, and cast, either—a competitor can go from winning the whole thing to being eliminated first the very next season, all depending on how the rules change. And don't even get me started on how individual wins are exponentially more difficult to achieve compared to team wins (and let's all agree that the *Champs vs. Pros/Stars* wins don't count the same as a regular-season or an *All Stars* win). With how much *The Challenge* has evolved over more than two decades, it's absolutely impossible to judge each champion by the same criteria.

The more you get into the debate, the more complicated it becomes to crown the *Challenge* GOAT—and that's exactly what makes it so much fun. From the diehard fans who spend hours discussing the show on social media every week to even the most casual of viewers who watched a few seasons back in the day when it wasn't even called *The Challenge* yet, everyone enjoys analyzing what it takes to win this wildly unpredictable game and who does it the best. As a longtime fan of *The Challenge* myself, I literally made a career out of doing just that. In my time covering the show for *Entertainment Weekly*, I've gotten to know many of the fan-favorite champs and underdogs, gaining a deeper understanding of what goes into making a winning strategy—and how difficult it is to actually pull it off. There's so much more to it than what you see on TV, because there are only so many minutes in each episode. And once all the players cross the finish line at the end of the final, the season may be over—but their story definitely isn't. Sometimes, the most epic and meaningful parts of a competitor's journey happen because they won, long after the cameras have stopped rolling. I've seen how winning *The Challenge* has changed people's lives in both subtle and massive ways that the show isn't able to capture on-screen for the fans.

That's how this book came to life. *How to Win at* The Challenge *and Life* peels back the curtain on aspects of the game that are impossible to display on the show, but fans like myself are still dying to know about—like the thought process that leads to creating a winning political strategy, or the secret to dominating physical challenges, or the trick to making the best alliance possible. No one becomes a *Challenge* champ on a fluke, and it turns out there's even more that goes into it than people may think. In this book, I interviewed some of the most accomplished, iconic, famous, and even infamous champions to discuss their time on and off *The Challenge*. As they share the secrets to their successes and explain how they won when so many others haven't, they also reveal how enduring the physical, mental, and emotional challenges and eventually winning the show influenced their lives outside the game in unexpected and inspiring ways.

From dominant physical competitors to slick political geniuses to players who just refused to give up in the face of insurmountable odds, no two philosophies, strategies, or experiences are the same. But what they all have in common is the same result—winning *The Challenge* changed their lives. And something that came as a surprise even to me after all the years

I've obsessively followed this show is how many of the lessons the champs learned from their time playing the game can be relevant for fans as well. Even though most of us will never find ourselves in situations like what these competitors go through, the hard-earned wisdom and messages the champs share are applicable to everyone's lives. And what is perhaps the most inspiring message of all is the way in which most of them consider their biggest failures or mistakes to be the most important part of their stories because of what they learned and how they grew from those negative experiences. Even the best of the best struggle sometimes, and they're sharing those vulnerable feelings here in the hopes that they can help others too.

Most of this book focuses on the history of twenty-one of the greatest *Challenge* champs of all time, but I also couldn't resist finding out how they feel about their futures on the show as well. We're talking about some of the most legendary winners of all time, and many of them haven't competed in years! In a perfect world, we'd see all of them return at some point to find out if they still have what it takes to dominate in this ever-evolving game (or even make my dream of an all-champ season come true—think of how epic that would be!). You'll have to see what each of them said about whether or not they're interested in coming back to find out how likely that is.

Whether you're reading this because you're a *Challenge* superfan looking for never-before-heard stories about your favorite seasons or players, or you're hoping to compete on the show one day and want to learn from the best on how to kick ass in the game, or you need some motivation for your own life, this book has it all. But that's enough from me—I'll let the champs take it from here.

THE ONE-TIME CHAMPS

CYNTHIA ROBERTS

Champion: *Road Rules: All Stars*

While Cynthia Roberts is one of the very first *Challenge* champions ever, winning in the traditional sense of the word was never her number one goal. In fact, winning her first season didn't have anything to do with beating her competition, succeeding in eliminations, working a flawless political strategy, or any other aspect of the game you'd now associate with being a champion. The *Real World: Miami* alum is one of only five people who competed on the very first season of *The Challenge* in 1998, and back then it was almost a completely different show. For one thing, *Road Rules: All Stars* didn't even have the words "The Challenge" in the title (that got added two seasons later). There was just one team of *Real World* alums who worked together to complete missions while driving around the United States and New Zealand in an RV. At the end of the season, they each walked away with an all-expenses-paid trip to Costa Rica as their prize, which was pretty sweet at the time. But the real prize Cynthia got that season was worth so much more.

"They say I'm a winner of a *Challenge*, and I'm like, 'Did I win, though?'" Cynthia says. "It wasn't an elimination-type thing; that didn't come until much later. There's big money involved now, but there wasn't back then. People are training to do these shows now, which I think is fantastic, but it's like this has turned into something way bigger than what we ever imagined. We were the pioneers; for us, it was humble beginnings. It was more being put in these situations that I would never even imagine I would be doing, and then also enjoying those things, which I never thought possible."

Cynthia didn't have any expectations when she agreed to go on *Road Rules: All Stars*. Still, nothing could have prepared the Bay Area native for what she experienced on the show and how it ended up changing her for good. "I had never traveled before, but I took a risk by doing this and I'm so glad that I did," she says. "Those experiences have developed me in a lot of ways to want to know more about the world, to want to be more, to want to experience more."

Even though her mother called her the risk-taker in her family when she was younger, never in a million years could she have predicted that one day she'd be jumping off the side of a skyscraper in New Zealand—and doing it while wearing sandals. "The one memory that stands out the most to me was when they brought us to one of the tallest buildings in the country and we had to scale down the side of it," she says. "They didn't tell us what the challenge was in advance, so I'm out there for some reason in freaking flip-flops. I honestly didn't think I could go through with it."

Cynthia remembers getting the harness on and freaking out as she looked down the side of the building. "I'm like, 'I don't even have the appropriate attire, I can't do this,'" she says. "'You're really expecting me to walk down the side of a building?' That doesn't seem like a big deal, but when you're in it and you're up there, the hardest part was to put yourself over the side of the ledge." There was only so much the safety team could do for her. Cynthia knew she had to take the final step herself, and it was one of the hardest things she's ever had to do . . . but she took a breath and just did it. She leaned over the side and made her descent. "My toes are holding on to the flip-flops, I'm scared to death, and I just remember hollering, 'Oh, Jesus,' all the way down. 'Oh, Lord. Oh, Jesus.' But coming down the side of the building, once I finally got down to the bottom, I felt so proud of myself. I think I might have even kissed the ground. I was so, so, so, so scared and I couldn't believe I would ever do something like that, but I did."

She'll never forget the exhilarating feeling she had that day—not from plummeting to the ground off the side of a skyscraper, although that was a once-in-a-lifetime feeling in itself, but rather from the knowledge that she pushed herself to do something so outside of her comfort zone. "All of a sudden, I realized that I could do anything if I put my mind to it," Cynthia says. "Also never say never to anything. You should try anything that comes along—that doesn't apply to drugs and stuff that will kill. But new experiences, do it even if it scares you. Because once you get to the other side of it, you just feel victorious."

Not every mission was as high-flying as that one, but Cynthia still pushed herself in each one, even when it led to what she calls the grossest experience she's ever had, when she had to milk cows and shear sheep on a farm. As a self-proclaimed city girl, even the idea of being near a cow was new. But she got more up close and personal with the animals than she ever wanted to be. "The footage is out there, and you will be in tears watching me on that dairy farm," she says with a laugh. "The smell was atrocious, and I'm already a super-duper ger-

One of the OG *Challenge* champs.

mophobe. We had to milk a cow, and it was the most disgusting thing I have ever had to do in my life, because cows will just start taking a shit anytime and there is no warning. I was, like, outside my body this whole time."

And don't even get her started on how shearing the sheep went. "They literally give me these clippers, and mind you, I've always had long nails. I'm very girly, right?" she says. "I'm out here with these long nails and they're trying to make me shear their sheep. I'm digging too deep so I'm nicking it. They had to turn the sheep over, holding his legs, and it got to the point where a person that worked there had to try to guide me to do it. I'm just dying, there's sheep hair everywhere, and the sheep is practically screaming, 'Baaah,' and it was a mess."

At this point, she knew she wasn't going to come out of the episode looking like a professional farmer. She fully expected to be the comedic relief with the way she was being filmed. And she laughs at how her friends love to watch the episode over and over to make fun of how much she was struggling. "Oh my god, I was dying. It was terrible," she says. "The camera crew are not supposed to be a part of this environment, but they are in tears laughing while I'm, like, having a fit. I'm not trying to be funny, but it ended up being really funny." Having one of her most embarrassing moments immortalized forever on TV was yet another terrifying prospect, and while Cynthia isn't exactly dying to show that episode to everyone in her life, she's glad she didn't let a little embarrassment stop her from experiencing something so vastly different from how she grew up. "At least I can say that I did that. Everyone can see that I did that. I could have easily walked away, but I didn't."

Road Rules: All Stars filmed over twenty years ago, but Cynthia has never forgotten how accomplished each of those experiences made her feel, and that's had a massive impact on her ever since. "My life before this wasn't as adventurous," she says. "And I knew that I had to share the experiences I had with my son. I wanted him to be out in the world and get exposed to things I never had in my upbringing. You never know what you're going to like or not like unless you try it, whether you're doing it on TV in front of millions of people or not, so I'm constantly getting him to try new things."

In addition to passing on to her son her open-minded approach to life, Cynthia has also noticed how her time on *The Challenge*—including her short-lived return on 2004's *Battle of the Sexes 2* before she was voted out early—benefited her in other positive ways. "It's shown me how to deal with different types of personalities and how to accept people for who they are and to be able to meet them where they're at," she says. "I mean, you don't like everyone you work with. Did I like every single roommate I ever lived with? Absolutely not. But when you're in a situation where you have to deal with them, you learn you can't change a person. It's certainly helped me be a more well-rounded individual by accepting people for who they are, being comfortable in my own skin, and not feeling like I need to hold grudges for the rest of my life."

That's why, when Cynthia got a call to return to the *Challenge* world after over twenty years for *All Stars 3*, she said yes—even though she knew nothing about how the franchise had evolved since she was last on. Her memories and what she learned from her first two seasons were so positive that she was open to seeing how this new experience would benefit her. That's not to say she wasn't shocked to get the invitation to return after so many years, though. "When they called me out of the blue, I said, 'You know I'm an old lady now, right?' And they laughed," she says. "I spend my time in an office at a desk or at home working on a computer all day long. I do have a full life, but it's certainly not jumping out of planes and climbing Mount Rushmore. That's not my life."

Cynthia hadn't kept up with watching *The Challenge* in the years since she was last on, so the biggest shock for her was how physical the game had gotten. "Back then, I didn't have to worry about wrestling nobody, and now I've been a mother a lot longer than most of these people have been doing these shows," she says. "Going back, my insecurity was mostly my ability to physically perform." But Cynthia knew that as long as she tried whatever was thrown her way and didn't let her fears get the best of her, she'd be fine no matter what happened. And while she didn't win her second *Challenge* championship on *All Stars 3*, she still walked away with a life-changing realization, just as she did on her first season. Ever since she got home from *All Stars 3*, after seeing what her fellow competitors could do physically, she's been inspired to work on her own fitness. "My sister is a personal trainer, and she's been training me every day ever since. And I feel fucking fantastic," Cynthia says. "It's never been about how I look on the outside, because I don't want to lose weight. I'm just trying to build muscle, build endurance, get my insides working better, because I spend so much time sitting at a desk in my daily life."

It's something her sister has been trying to get her to do for years, but it wasn't until *All Stars 3* that she learned the importance of keeping herself healthy by working out regularly. "It took me all this time and for this experience to come up and for me to understand that just a little bit of working out every day is so important," Cynthia says. "I'm more focused now. I feel happier. I have more energy. And I never would have known that if not for *The Challenge*."

ALTON WILLIAMS

Champion: *The Gauntlet 2*

When it comes to the physical part of *The Challenge*, Alton Williams is one of the best in the game. He beat his opponents so definitively in eliminations and challenges that it was almost embarrassing for anyone who dared go against him. It seemed as if no one could best the *Real World: Las Vegas* alum in any kind of one-on-one matchup. Have you seen the guy climb a net? He defied the laws of physics with how fast he flew up one on *The Gauntlet 2*. It was a champion-making performance, and Alton deservedly got his first and only *Challenge* win from that season. With four appearances on the main franchise and one season of the *All Stars* spin-off, he made every final except one, and that kind of winning record is rare. But Alton cares more about his one elimination loss than anything else because of how it happened, and what it taught him about himself.

"What motivates me is not to be the best, but rather the opportunity to suck and to then strategically figure it out," Alton says. "Everything in my life is always so preplanned. I'm like a Boy Scout. So to go into an environment that's completely unplanned by me and that's made to purposely be harder for me in particular is exciting." That's what made competing on *The Challenge* fulfilling for Alton—it gave him the chance to push himself in ways he'd never done before. "I would volunteer to go first in challenges and then be the only one who could do it, and it was not as good of a show for them. There's this thing they came up with called 'the Alton effect,' which is any way production makes sure that I'm not going to be the only one to get something done."

When he made his reality TV debut on *The Real World: Las Vegas* in 2002, Alton had no idea it would lead to him making a name for himself as a top physical competitor on *The Challenge*. "I'd never watched the show before," he says. "It was just a new opportunity. My mom's a soap opera actress, so I knew television as a way to exist, and maybe that tuned me to it, but I never really wanted to do that. I'm more into veterinary medicine, horses, being outside, hunting, that kind of thing. I'm a really spiritual person, and I set my goals and then I let life guide me toward that."

At that time, he was twenty-two and had just decided to stop being a professional skater after a painful injury. He still had a drive to do something active, however, so when he and his *Real World* castmate/girlfriend Irulan Wilson were invited to join the cast of *The Gauntlet*, he realized that was the perfect path. "But I learned it's not great to bring a girlfriend on a *Challenge*, because I spent a lot of time protecting her and being caught up in her drama," he says. "I realized that it was probably best to just separate that kind of stuff." While he hated the drama, he loved the physical aspect of the game. "I quickly realized it's one of those things where being big and strong doesn't matter. I think being a surfer was better training. There's something about *The Challenge* that brings everything into balance. Everybody's on the same playing field, and it's more about internal grit."

Surprisingly, Alton is the first to admit that he doesn't have that certain mental edge that he thinks is essential for being a top *Challenge* competitor. "That's one thing I really learned. I'm blessed in certain things, I have certain talents, but I don't have that competitive spirit," he says. "I'm just going to run my race and do the best that I can. I think that I always went into the challenges and messed up the dynamic a little bit, because I came in there with such a pure camp spirit, which is kind of weird. I'm a really good competitor, but at the same time, I'm oblivious to what's going on within the game. It's like showing up to a football game with soccer equipment, and everyone's like, 'What is going on? That's our star quarterback.' I've always felt like that."

During his rookie season on *The Gauntlet*, Alton absolutely destroyed Laterrian Wallace in a pole climbing elimination—it wasn't even close. He eventually made it to the final, but his *Real World* team ended up losing to the *Road Rules* team. "After that, I learned that everybody is afraid—I don't care how big they are, how strong their muscles are, how many veins they got popping out of their neck—the whole thing's run by fear and every strategy is run by fear," Alton says. "All you have to do is just flip that on its head and be assertive." That experience inspired him to volunteer for eliminations in future seasons, even when he was safe, which is almost unheard of on *The Challenge*. "I'm a protector, and I know whoever is standing there is scared, so I think this is a great opportunity for me to jump in there and to change the game. I would just wait for the energy and then I'd say, 'Yes, today's not a day where I'm standing around on the side.' And I jump in there with such an energy that it's impossible to lose. I will send them home unapologetically."

Most players do anything and everything they can to avoid eliminations, but Alton found himself eager to do as many as possible, despite how unpredictable each individual game is. "I'm wily, I'm really creative, I'm good at figuring out the game first," he says. "You can't wait until you're up there in order to figure out what you're going to be doing, which is what most people do. You have to get your toes ready, loosen up your hips. Usually my strategy was just, 'Does it feel fun? Heck yeah, let's go.' That's it. If it feels fun, I'm going to win. And it was never against a weaker person. I usually like to go against somebody I think is going to win."

By the time Alton arrived for his second season, *The Gaunt-let 2*, he had no doubt in his mind that he was going to win this time. "Just with our team, and I knew that the show didn't know who I was yet, they didn't know what they're up against," he says. "I was going to win. The first season, I had [Mike] 'the Miz' [Mizanin] there and I just played the background because I had a girlfriend. The second time, I just broke up with Irulan, we were on this island in Tobago, so it was very spiritual—I'd never really had a spiritual experience, and I experienced something visceral where the clouds opened and I felt the energy type of thing and you're like, 'Oh, crap, we're going to win this thing.'"

He started the season off on a strong note, outlasting all the other men in a battle royale to become captain of the Rookies team. He won three impressive eliminations that solidified his reputation as a physical beast, and eventually won the final, earning his first *Challenge* championship. When he returned for *The Inferno 3*, he lived up to the name of his Good Guys

Nets, ropes . . . how does Alton make climbing things look so easy?

team and threw himself into an elimination to save Davis Mallory from having to compete. Alton won that elimination against Tyrie Ballard, and while he made it to another final, his team lost in the end.

After a five-year break from the show, Alton returned for 2012's *Battle of the Seasons*, but he immediately found himself struggling with how much the social and political game had evolved in the time he'd been away. He quickly realized that he no longer enjoyed the competition like he used to. Plus, he butted heads with a lot of the younger, more aggressive cast members who were trying to make a name for themselves in the new era of *The Challenge*, and the house dynamics became uncomfortable for him. "It's always been more about the relationships than winning for me, and when I see people suffering, I want to help, and then I see the people who are perpetrating it and I'm like, 'Leave them alone,' and the next thing you know, I lose half my friends," Alton says. "I've had the horrible experience of having the whole house go against me, which I think was a great experience, actually. Most people's biggest fear is to be unliked, and they'll do ridiculous things for a lifetime to try not to experience that. In Turkey, having the whole house go against me and realizing that it was my fault, it was really interesting going through that experience."

It was a very emotional time for Alton, as he was grieving the loss of his father at the same time. "I really needed love, and I realized that this is an inner game, just like life is an inner game," he says. "On *The Challenge*, I realized that as competitive as I was, it's more of a mental choice to be more aware of what's going on inside of me than involved in the game. This was a really special opportunity for me to figure myself out and be in a place where people aren't answering to me—I'm the boss in every world that I'm in, I'm one of the heads of my family, I'm the oldest of fourteen siblings and I put them through college, took care of my mom, and I'm still doing it to this day. I went from a place where I was respected in my family into *The Challenge*, where I was the enemy because I'm in the middle of somebody else's pursuit of success."

Alton found himself in the center of a lot of drama that season after he had a brief showmance with Sarah Rice. "It was gnarly," he says. "They called my room 'the church,' and in the first week or two, everybody came to the room, and it was very spiritual. It was great—they would come just to drink tea and chill, read books and stuff. And then the room turned into the place where you go to be ostracized, and I was ostracized from the house and from my own team because I was hooking up with Sarah. That really got me in trouble with Trishelle [Cannatella] and with Nany [González]." The Las Vegas team also fought over who they should make an alliance with, which put

Alton at odds with Frank Fox (formerly Sweeney) and Zach Nichols from the San Diego team. "I liked them the first two weeks there, but then they transitioned into their mean-boy strategy. And then me and Dustin [Zito] had a falling-out that last night, and I just realized I wasn't in with my team anymore."

After bonding with Robb Schreiber from the St. Thomas team, Alton felt bad that Robb was about to go against him in an elimination. "It was his first *Challenge*, and he was getting ready to go home because he was going against me," Alton says. "I was like, 'F this, man. I'm not going to be this kid's stumbling block. I'll go home and continue veterinary medicine and continue with my businesses. I don't want to be here.' I wrote a letter to him saying, 'Try your hardest, make me look good.' And that was it." Alton decided to lose the elimination on purpose, even though that meant ending his winning streak, as well as taking Nany down with him. "Nany wasn't my friend anyway, so I didn't care, quite frankly."

During the elimination, Alton was shocked that he and Nany still almost beat Robb and Marie Roda, even though he wasn't trying to win. "I slowed it down because I did not want to go back to that house," he says. "I wouldn't say I threw it. They had to win. But they were competing against Nany and a quarter of me. I knew, 'This is going to be my last time. I'm totally not for this type of world anymore.'"

He didn't return to *The Challenge* for almost ten years after that, despite getting some offers. "I realized that I've done everything on *Challenge*s," he says. He confirmed that feeling after deciding to give it one last shot on the first season of the *All Stars* spin-off in 2021. He won another elimination, made another final, and finished in sixth place, but what he remembers most from that season is his showmance with Jisela Delgado and the drama it caused with a significant other at home. "I thought that I was broken up, but I guess we weren't. I didn't understand this girl's dynamic so well," Alton says. "And then I went on *The Challenge* and they quarantined us for a long time, and being from such a big family, I'm not used to being alone. Then getting turned loose into this *Challenge* house, and there's a beautiful girl there and she's showing me attention, and I haven't had that kind of beautiful attention in a long time, I got caught up in that and ended up falling in like with that feeling with Jisela. But I come to find out, a lot of that wasn't as organic as I felt."

Alton believes he could have won *All Stars*, but he ruined it. "It was my show, but what happened was Jisela, and then I put that feeling in my stomach because I knew that it was going to go bad for me in my real world, and there's no happy ending to an unhappy journey," he says. "I should've just stayed with my boys, and oh my god, it would've been a great show." He also regrets not volunteering for eliminations like he'd done in previous seasons. "That is what I messed up on: I literally could have sent everyone home. They were expecting me to volunteer and literally start pointing people out, and I would've sent that season's winner Yes [Duffy] home. But I tried to be a little different than Mr. Superman who was on every show, jumping up, and it ended up costing me."

Despite how grueling the two-day final was on *All Stars*, it ended up being exactly what Alton needed at that time. "I literally almost quit right in the middle of the final, no question about it," he says. "I was done, and then something came over me. It was just a question. 'Can you make it another step? Can you make it another mile? Can you get to the top of that hill? Will you make it to that tree over there?' And it was only because I have quit a show before once and that cost me a lot mentally. There was a quitter in me, and it exposed itself in Turkey and it stayed with me in the real world." Finishing the final and proving that he had what it takes to persevere turned out to be a better reward than another championship. "I don't really need to go race for somebody else's five hundred thousand dollars."

Five seasons of victories, triumphs, and, yes, even quitting on *The Challenge* have changed Alton in ways he never expected. "I've learned a lot about myself, and I would say I'm definitely a better person just from seeing myself in that light. I don't think enough people get to really look at themselves through other people's eyes, and I think the show really helped that for me. It's a very different energy you give when you have that confidence. I'm very comfortable with me."

JULIE ROGERS

Champion: *Extreme Challenge*

All Julie Rogers (formerly Stoffer) wants to do is compete on *The Challenge* again. The *Real World: New Orleans* alum won the first season she was on, *Extreme Challenge* in 2001, but in the decades since, she hasn't been able to get a second championship. It's not for lack of trying—she returned for four more seasons after that, and even made it to the final on her last season. Still, Julie's experience is vastly different from most *Challenge* champions' in that, as soon as she achieved success on the show, things only got worse from there. But over twenty years later, she still hasn't given up trying to change how her story ends. "I know I have the physical ability to win another one," Julie says. "And whether you win or lose, *The Challenges* are just so fun. Heck, I'll go as an alternate, I'm not joking. I just want to be involved again."

Julie's reality TV career didn't start on a positive note, either. "I was that Mormon girl who got kicked out of college for going on *The Real World*," she says. During her junior year at Brigham Young University, she read an article in her school's newspaper about auditions for *The Real World*. When she got cast on the show, she knew it would be a complicated situation, since the Mormon school had rules against men and women living together. She thought deferring for the amount of time it would take to film a season of *The Real World* would protect her from breaking any "purity" rules. "I thought, they're not really going to kick me out of school, considering I'm being filmed twenty-four-seven, and obviously, I'm not having sex with people. I left that show as virginal as I came into it. I only kissed people, but it was enough for the Mormons, because if you're a woman and you're Mormon, you're supposed to be as pure as the driven snow. I couldn't be kissing people or even living in the same house with them."

After her season of *The Real World* finished shooting, Julie's only plan was to try to get cast on *The Challenge*, both to fulfill a dream of competing and to buy herself some time to figure out the next chapter in her life. "I've been kicked out of college, I don't have a degree, and I wanted to do *Challenge*s as soon as I found out what they were because I was really into the competition part of it," she says. Julie and her *Real World* castmate Jamie Murray were invited to compete on *Extreme Challenge* together, and the experience was everything she'd hoped it would be. "That was definitely the best *Challenge* I've ever been on. We went to Europe, we did all this fun stuff across America. It was just amazing. And then we won, so it was an awesome taste of victory."

Throughout that season, Julie and Jamie formed a close relationship. "We ended up kind of hooking up," she says. "We had a bond on *The Real World*, and *The Challenge* was such an intense experience. But there was nothing romantic. I think our friendship just got deeper. But really, Jamie and I have never had any romantic feelings for each other, we just connected because we both have interest in the metaphysical, unconventional spiritual realm." She pauses. "And then just the fact that we're both fucking crazy and like to do crazy shit."

Their friendship ended up changing the course of the rest of her *Challenge* career in ways she never could have predicted. Julie believes that her former *Real World* roommate Melissa Beck (formerly Howard) had feelings for Jamie and became jealous of Julie's friendship with him. She points to her experience on *Battle of the Sexes* in 2002, when Melissa orchestrated Julie's exit at the beginning of the season. "Of course, she does everything she can to get me voted off first," Julie says.

She returned for *The Inferno* in 2004 hoping that the slate had been wiped clean and she could compete this time. But she felt as if everyone already judged her without getting to know her after *Battle of the Sexes*. "I would have enemies that I didn't even know I had," she says. "If *The Challenge* was a physical thing only, I know I would win. But then you add this element of years of drama, and I couldn't beat it."

Things went from bad to worse during a daily challenge that season when Julie and Veronica Portillo were hanging from zip lines, and Julie tugged on the back of Veronica's safety harness. Veronica thought Julie was trying to unclip her harness and freaked out in a moment that's become one of the most iconic *Challenge* clips of all time, and Julie added the nickname "Mormon Murderer" to her reputation.

"I didn't try to murder Veronica, okay?" Julie says with a laugh. "First of all, I'm scared of heights, and I'm just trying to win. I thought the game was pull the flag or something, and I'm grabbing on to her safety line. There were *two* safety lines;

the show's not trying to get anybody killed. No one's getting mortally injured and certainly no one's died, and I think that's a testament to certainly I could never have killed Veronica. I wasn't trying to undo any of our safety lines. But we were both scared shitless, way high up in the air, and I was being kind of aggressive. I take things a little bit far sometimes." She says she doesn't hold a grudge against Veronica for how the nickname has followed her around for twenty years. "I'm fine with it. It works for me, because guess what? I got called on more *Challenge*s because of that, so thank you, Veronica."

After that incident with Veronica, any hope Julie had of turning her social capital around that season instantly disappeared. "I have a lot of drive and ambition to win these things, and I always bring one hundred and ten percent every time, to the point that people think that I'm trying to murder people on *Challenge*s," she says. "All the women started freaking out because they're like, 'Oh my god, this woman is so insane. She's trying to murder me.' I'm trying to win. This is called competition."

Julie was eventually selected to go into an elimination against Katie Cooley (formerly Doyle) and lost, and she's still upset over how that played out. "I love Katie, she's amazing, but she was totally a chain-smoker at the time, and the challenge was running on a treadmill," Julie says. "Listen, I've run cross-country my whole life. I can run an eight-minute mile and I can run a half marathon. It's not a problem. This is my thing. But they never turned the treadmill up, so it was a walking pace the whole time."

The elimination was meant to continue until one player outlasted the other, and in the event of a tie, they had to jump rope instead. "They were trying to make it look like she and

I are in kind of a competition on a treadmill, which we are not, because anybody can walk on a treadmill," she says. "If they would've turned it up, it would've been over. We start jump-roping, and I trip on it immediately. That's it. Now I'm eliminated."

When she returned for *The Inferno II*, she produced yet another iconic clip when she went against her Good Guys team's advice and attempted to ride a motorized minibike across a short, narrow bridge rather than take the longer, safer route. While chanting, "The road to God is straight and narrow," she immediately fell into the water and forfeited the challenge for her team. "I've failed at certain challenges that I was just heartbroken about, including that one in particular," she says. "I was just sure I was going to do it. And I failed my team." She immediately went into an elimination as a result and lost to Tonya Cooley.

Julie tried to win one last time on *The Gauntlet 2*, and for the first time since her rookie season, she actually made it all the way to the end. But the Veterans team lost to the Rookies in the final. "I was there with Jamie again, but I was competing against Jamie, and I did get close to winning," she says. "But Jamie won and I lost, all because my team couldn't eat a burrito. No joke. The big final challenge was a burrito-eating contest and I was literally making myself throw up my breakfast so I'd have room for the burrito, but we didn't get it done. Otherwise, I would have won that *Challenge*."

She wasn't ready to call it quits on her *Challenge* career just yet after that close call, which is why she was disappointed when she stopped getting invited back after *The Gauntlet 2*. "That first win on *The Challenge* was huge for me, because the car I won, I lived in it for a while," she says. Even though she never got her second win, she's still grateful for all the experiences she had on the show—even all the negative ones. "Interestingly enough, it still made my life better in a lot of ways, because I have been the target of some serious mean-girl stuff, and these are very dramatic life experiences to be having. Then you go back to your normal life, and everything is cool, because nothing compares to the intensity of these situations you were in. It makes everything else in life super easy to deal with. When stuff starts feeling heavy, I'll just be like, 'Oh yeah. But remember *The Challenge*? In comparison to some of the crazy shit I've done on *The Challenge*, this isn't that bad.' You become a strong-ass individual after multiple *Challenge*s."

In the years since she last appeared on *The Challenge*, Julie got married and became a mother. Now she lives with her family in the Midwest, where she works in real estate. Her current life couldn't be further from her reality TV world, and that's exactly how she likes it. "On these shows, I'm a character," she says. "In my real life, my husband, my family, my friends don't even call me Julie. I separate my life from this, and I don't really identify with the character that ended up being portrayed."

That being said, if *The Challenge* ever came knocking on her door again, she'd say yes in a heartbeat. She recently filmed *The Real World Homecoming: New Orleans* reunion special for Paramount+, but her ultimate goal is to get cast on a season of the *All Stars* spin-off. "They were supposed to have me on the first *All Stars*," she says. "I had my contract signed, and I hired my nanny and was ready to go." Unfortunately, the production team made a last-minute casting change, and Julie's dream of returning to *The Challenge* was put on hold. She hasn't given up hope for a future season, though. "Anything I can do to get back on a *Challenge*, I'll try, because I will win. I do construction for a living. I teach yoga. I'll get back into CrossFit. Victory has been so close—I got a taste of it, and I would like a chance again. I don't necessarily need money, but I want the glory. Now it's just about the game."

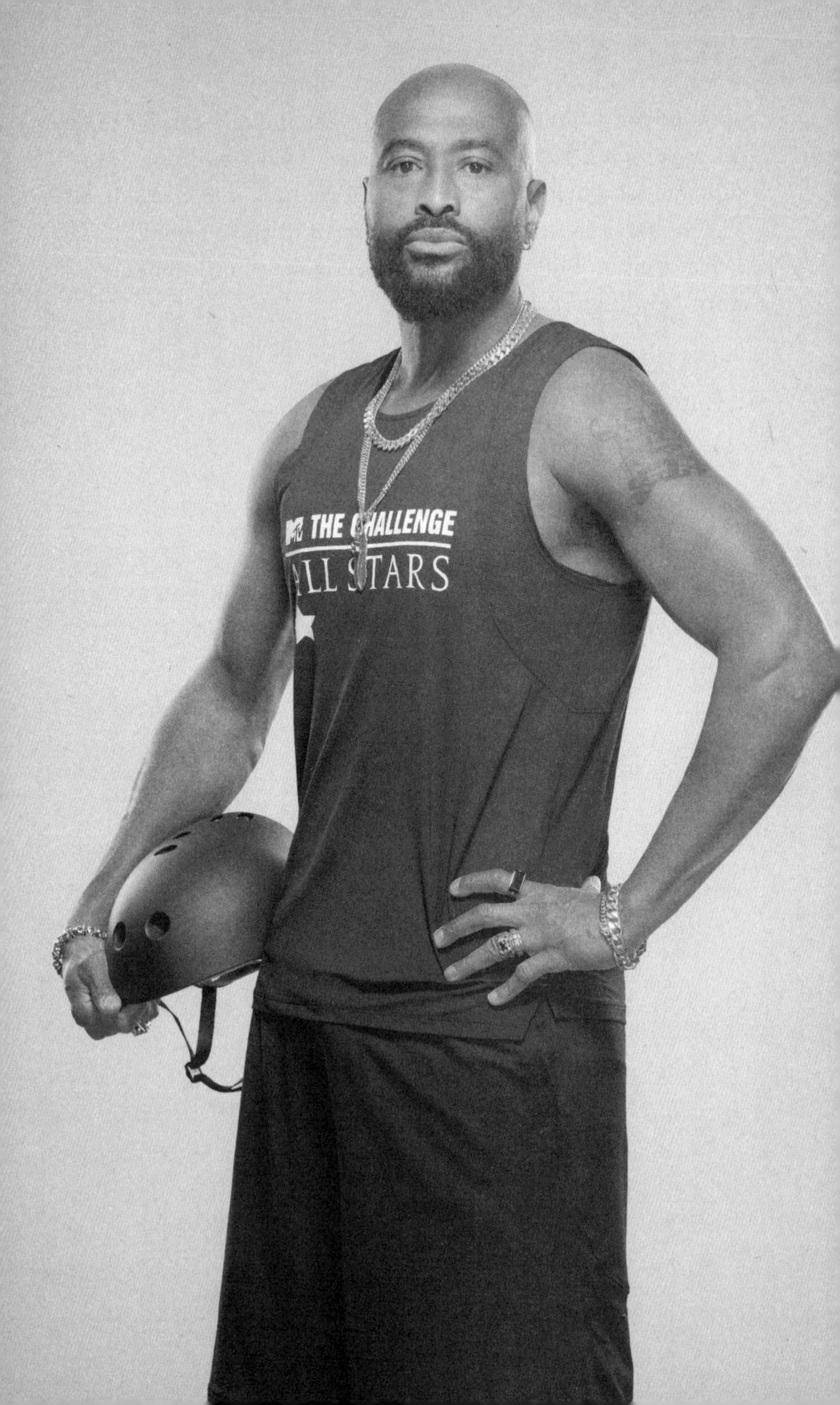
THE CHALLENGE
ALL STARS

SYRUS YARBROUGH

Champion: *Extreme Challenge*

Syrus Yarbrough doesn't just want to win—he always *expects* to win. That's how he approaches everything in his life, not just on *The Challenge*. And while the *Real World: Boston* alum won the first season of *The Challenge* he competed on in 2001, the moments in which he *didn't* win on the show since then are what's changed his life in more meaningful ways. "In all those years on *The Challenge*, I've embraced the good and the bad, in the game, out of the game, and at home," Syrus says. "As long as I'm showing growth, I think I'm fine. And that's in *The Challenge* or in real life. It's a progressive thing for me."

Thriving in unexpected ways has always been a trend in his life. It began when he was growing up, when he realized that he didn't fit people's preconceived notions of him. "Being a Black male, you carry the weight of culture on your shoulders," Syrus says. "I will always be outspoken because racism will not stand, so people look at me and think I'm this crazy, militant, Black power dude, but I'm not. I'm a big advocate for mental health; I've sought help out since the tenth grade." And the story of how Syrus wound up on *The Challenge* is especially atypical.

While most reality TV stars audition for shows with the intention of being on camera, Syrus was actually trying to get a job behind the scenes on *The Real World*. "I got on the show by mistake," he says with a laugh. "I had just graduated college. I had done everything that life had told me to do, and then life smacked me and I wasn't able to get a job."

In his attempts to work on the crew, Syrus ended up getting chosen as a cast member instead for *The Real World: Boston* in 1997. It wasn't what he'd intended, but he seized on the opportunity to find success via this new, unexpected path. He changed up his appearance in preparation to introduce what would become his iconic look: "I had dreadlocks, and cutting off my hair was all part of me being twenty-five and going on the show and knowing and understanding what branding was. I rode that wave for so long, and I got people to respect what it was I [brought] to the table."

The Challenge didn't exist yet when Syrus was filming his season of *The Real World*, but he and his fellow castmates became the unofficial first Challengers when they took a trip to Puerto Rico. "*Road Rules* was island hopping that year, and they ended up coming to Puerto Rico and sent us a note saying they wanted to challenge us to some games in the rain forest," Syrus says. "That's pretty much how the whole concept of *The Challenge* was started. We kicked their butts in the rain forest and won that." It was Syrus's first taste of reality TV competition, and he was hooked—he literally bled to get the win. "I blew my shin wide open, and it was so bad. I was a mess, but I'll do anything for the competition. It definitely was one to remember."

Syrus had such a blast during that mini-*Challenge* that when he saw other *Real World* and *Road Rules* alums getting cast on a real version of *The Challenge* (then known as *Road*

Rules: All Stars) that premiered a year later, he was mad that he didn't get an invitation for the first three seasons. When he finally got the call to go on the fourth season, *Extreme Challenge*, he didn't hesitate to say yes even though he wasn't in the best physical shape at the time. "I was getting paid ungodly amounts of money to host nightclubs, and I would do sometimes three clubs in a night," he says. "It was the craziest time in my life, sitting there with a forty in hand, double cheeseburger dripping with everything. I was a mess, out of shape, and overweight."

When he arrived on *Extreme Challenge*, he was relieved to find out that—at least, back then—he didn't need to be in great shape to win. "It was so much more than just physical. It was all-encompassing," he says. "*The Challenge* tests you mentally, physically, emotionally, and then sees what you've got when it comes to your drive. It's tough. And then you got to deal with all these personalities on top of that. And then you got to have a political game, too. On the earlier *Challenge*s, we were trying to figure things out as we went."

The *Real World* team won the majority of the challenges that season, and Syrus credits their success to having a well-rounded group of people who refused to lose by sheer force of will. "Truly, our cast wasn't made up of a bunch of competitors," he says. "We won the whole thing because we had people from all walks of life on our team. At least half of us did not enjoy heights or speed, were claustrophobic, wouldn't eat anything, and it was all that stuff. But we still did it. I am so scared of heights, and the first thing we did was bungee jump into a ring of fire. And guess what production does? They mess up, so I've got to do it again. I had to do it *twice*. That's *The Challenge*: be ready for any- and everything at all times. I'll never forget that."

Syrus is proud that he didn't back down from anything that season, even when he was pushed out of his comfort zone. "Should I have been out there doing some of the stuff I was doing? Probably not," he says with a laugh. "But that's part of the fun of it. I want to be able to tell friends and kids and fans, 'I was terrified, but I did it.' For me, it's about the competition just as much as it is the money. I'd be doing the same damn thing if money was not involved."

After winning *Extreme Challenge*, Syrus returned to compete on *Battle of the Sexes*, *The Inferno*, *The Gauntlet 2*, *The Ruins*, and the first and third seasons of *All Stars*, but he has yet to get his second *Challenge* championship. What he gained from those subsequent seasons instead were valuable lessons in patience and acceptance. When he faced off with Derrick Kosinski in a brutal physical elimination on *The Gauntlet 2*, host T.J. Lavin made a judgment call giving Derrick a point over Syrus—and things got heated. "When I almost got in that fight with T.J., it's because of my passion," he says. "I know Derrick's right arm was out before I was out, and they even show that on the replay, so I had a reason to be angry." While Syrus didn't agree with the ruling, he had to learn to accept it regardless. "There's a difference between playing sports where there's rules, and then there's *The Challenge*, which is a whole different beast. This is for entertainment. *The Challenge* is a television show. And I know that made great TV."

Syrus doesn't blame Derrick for what happened, and he also gives his opponent major credit for defeating him in the intense wrestling match despite being so much smaller than Syrus. "That was a really long fight, and he's very strong and fast. He's the pit bull for a reason," Syrus says. "He whupped my ass, let's get that out there. I lost. I'm okay with that. I could hear his neck cracking and popping when I would fall with his head under my arm. And he kept going. Kudos to him for keeping going. That dude's a boss. He deserved to win."

Another tough loss Syrus faced happened on *The Ruins* in 2009. He'd already won an elimination against Adam King that season, but he found himself back in an elimination shortly after, this time against Cohutta Grindstaff. Syrus and Cohutta were suspended by their wrists and ankles under a large log, and they had to make their way down to the opposite end, use a key to unlock their wrists and ankles, and then hit a gong. Syrus initially had a lead but ended up losing to Cohutta. "I clearly crushed him in the physical part, but then I couldn't get out of the shackles," Syrus says. "I went to one arm, the other arm, one leg, the other leg. And by that time, he caught up, and went on to undo one arm and one leg, and he rang the bell. But it is what it is. I can't change what happened. All I can ask for is another chance at it."

He didn't get that chance for a long time. After *The Ruins*, it wasn't until the first season of the *All Stars* spin-off in 2021 that he finally returned to *The Challenge*. He was doing well in the competition until he accidentally sprained his ankle while walking around outside the house in Argentina, and that injury cost him. He and Beth Stolarczyk competed in an elimination against Alton Williams and Aneesa Ferreira that required a lot of jumping up and down, and while Syrus never gave up despite the pain, they ended up losing.

Syrus does hold a grudge against Alton for how his game ended—he believes he was "set up" to get sent into elimination by Alton, who gassed out during that daily challenge despite never showing any kind of physical weakness in past seasons, making their team lose. "All I can ask for is another shot at it. I would love a one-on-one against Alton, in anything," he says. But despite that, he still considers that season to be a win because of how he was able to help Beth rehab her image after decades of being seen as one of the original reality TV villains. "Beth and I are actually really close friends, and people need to know that she's a beautiful person. She got the bad end of the stick for a long time. I told her, 'We are going to reinvent you on this *Challenge*, because you're going to be *you* for once. I got your back. People will finally see exactly what I see in you.' And that made that *Challenge* for me, personally. I feel like I've accomplished something going there with her and having her back with that."

When it comes to his own image from that season, however, Syrus is less than thrilled. Seeing how he looked in his cast photo from *All Stars* inspired him to make some big life changes. "Oh my god, that picture haunts me," he says. It was the motivation Syrus needed to get back into better shape, and now when he compares his *All Stars* headshot with the more recent one from *All Stars 3*, he can't help but smile. "It's almost cry-worthy thinking about going back on *The Challenge* and getting myself back. I have goose bumps right now thinking about it. It's that crazy." Returning to *The Challenge* after over a decade also made Syrus realize just how precious these opportunities are, and he decided he's not going to waste any more of them. "I understand that this thing is almost over in my life because I'm fifty. But I'm going to give it my best shot in the last chapter. This is the fourth quarter. This is it. And I get a little emotional, the older I've gotten, understanding that the end of that journey is here."

He's not ready to call it quits just yet, though. Syrus is eager to compete on as many seasons of *The Challenge* as he can now that he's overhauled his fitness and gotten back into fighting shape. "Making the shift into Syrus 5.0, I'm in the gym every day," he says. "I do twenty miles a day on the damn bikes. I'm back with my six-pack. I'm fifty-six pounds lighter. I'm in optimal shape. I feel better than ever and I'm going to win a *Challenge* again." He's not just talking about *All Stars*, either—Syrus wants to be cast on the main franchise again to show the new, younger stars how it's done. "I want to go for the million. The excitement and the life that *All Stars* has helped pump back in me is a whole other level. I'm glowing. I don't have bad days. I'm better than ever, and I'm ready to show it."

EMILY SCHROMM

Champion: *Rivals II* (plus *Champs vs. Stars*)

Emily Schromm's *Challenge* career is relatively short, with only three seasons on the main franchise and one spin-off. But she has accomplished more in that time than most competitors could ever dream of. Out of four seasons, she won twice—*Rivals II* in 2013 and *Champs vs. Stars* in 2017. Of the two seasons she didn't win—*Cutthroat* in 2010 and *Battle of the Exes* in 2012—she finished third in both finals. She's undefeated in eliminations, earning her the reputation of a *Challenge* beast. But if a younger version of Emily saw the person she'd become after a few seasons of reality TV, she wouldn't even recognize herself.

Part of that is because Emily was raised in a fundamentalist Christian cult. "MTV was blocked in my house, and I didn't even know what reality TV was," she says. When she was discovered working in a Starbucks at her college, she and her mom googled *The Real World* to see what it was about, and during that initial Internet research, Emily learned about *The Challenge*—and she instantly fell in love with the adventure *The Challenge* offered. So she begged her mom to let her join the cast of *The Real World: DC* in 2009, only so that she could eventually make the transition over to *The Challenge*. "That was always the end goal for me, to get to something that was about athleticism and fun and travel. That was so much more of my scene than just living in the house with strangers."

Emily grew up playing soccer and other types of team sports, though she was never a particularly competitive person—or so she thought. So she had no idea what to expect when she arrived in Prague for *Cutthroat*. "The first conversation I had with Derrick [Kosinski], we were filming the big intro and we were in the car together waiting for our turn to drive around and get our shot," she says. "And I asked him, 'How do you know if you're going to be any good at these challenges?' And he's like, 'You don't.'" Emily realized that she was going to either perform well or get sent home, and she was nervous but excited to see if she could hack it. "What I liked about *The Challenge* is that if you don't pull your own weight, it's very obvious. And in eliminations, it's just you versus one other person, so it was the first time I got to experience one-on-one sports. [The outcome] was totally up to me."

But what she didn't foresee was what *The Challenge* would bring out in her. "It very quickly triggered this thing in me where I was so ready to prove to myself that I could do anything that got thrown at me," Emily says. "It just flipped a switch in me that I didn't even know I had. I didn't know I was that competitive. I didn't know I had that type of energy where there's no stopping. I learned so much about myself and who I was and what I was capable of and worked through so much self-doubt."

It took some time for her to learn how to harness that competitive drive, however. "The first *Challenge*, I had no idea what I was doing," Emily admits. She spent her time learning from her veteran teammates, mainly Derrick, Johnny "Bananas" Devenanzio, and Jenn Grijalva. "At that time, Derrick was really into CrossFit, so he would put us through workouts. Johnny was always giving advice on strategy. Jenn was really into nutrition, so she was teaching me about supplements—now I have my own supplement line. It was all these little, tiny nuggets from these experienced veterans that changed everything for me."

That was how she learned that she wasn't physically ready for what it took to win a *Challenge*—at least, not yet. "It was before I was going to the gym consistently; it was before I really knew body awareness. I was so unprepared," she says. She remembers one day that season, Derrick gave her a pre-workout supplement for the first time in her life, and her whole body almost shut down mid-challenge. "I couldn't even think, I was so jittery. And when I started swimming, both of my legs cramped up so hard, it was so painful and I was swimming with just my arms. I was like, 'Oh my god, I'm so out of shape. This is not okay.' I realized that if I was going to ever do this again, I needed to get my shit together."

After placing third in the *Cutthroat* final with her teammate, Jenn—against two larger teams of four and five players—Emily went home and completely overhauled her lifestyle. "I wanted to understand what it's like to really know my body," she says. "I was already really unhealthy, drinking too much, smoking too much, and it got me focused on finding out what I can do if I'm disciplined and commit to something. That's how I got into powerlifting and exploring how far my body could go." While she initially began improving her fitness to do better on *The Challenge*, it ended up changing her life in even bigger and better ways. "I was so stuck in thinking about what my body *looked* like for most of my teenage years, and I had a lot of eating disorders because of that. Through *The Challenge*s and through fitness and empowering myself, I cared so much more about the athletic Emily than I did about 'getting to be a certain figure' Emily. 'What am I capable of?' rather than 'What do I look like?' That transformed me in my early twenties as I created a really healthy relationship with food and with my body and with self-love."

By reevaluating her relationship with food, she realized she needed to make sure she had what her body needed while filming *The Challenge* rather than just relying on production to feed her. "I figured out what I needed to do to take care of myself in the house, and that meant I had to bring so much food," she says. "Half my suitcase was actually food and supplements and protein bars and peanut butter, because I just needed nutrients if I was actually going to make it through the whole season. I had to completely take care of myself and feed my mind, body, and spirit, and sometimes the only food they would have would be KFC. I hadn't eaten gluten in three years, and I ate it and it was just horrific, I was so sick. I had to look out for myself."

When she returned for *Battle of the Exes* in 2012, she was now ready to win in ways that she didn't know were possible back before *Cutthroat*. But she was thrown for a loop when she learned the theme of the season and that she was going to be partnered up with her ex. "I was like, 'Wait, I don't even have an ex,'" she says. She was shocked to learn she'd be paired with her *Real World* castmate Ty Ruff, with whom she'd made out twice during the first week of filming. She definitely didn't think he counted as an ex, but she was still excited to work with him on *The Challenge*—until she realized that he didn't have the same competitive drive to win that she recently discovered in herself. "There were so many moments where I would see Ty want to check out. It was only because of our friendship that he was not going to quit, not because he wanted to win it for himself. I'll forever hold him dear to my heart because he didn't give up and he pulled through for me."

After getting thrown into elimination three out of eight times that season (plus two times her rookie season), Emily had started to make a name for herself as a physical threat when she emerged victorious every time. She credits all her elimination successes to keeping her eye on the prize, no matter who her opponent was. "I realized I have to take the person out of it, just block it all out and show up," she says. "Like with Melinda [Collins, formerly Stolp] or Paula [Beckert, formerly Meronek], it was just a matter of making sure that I didn't look at her face while I was pushing her. Just focus on the end goal, which is getting back to your team and winning. It does feel like life or death. It's crazy how intense and primal it is, but it teaches you more about yourself than anything."

On *Battle of the Exes*, getting thrown in week after week lit a new kind of fire in Emily, this time as the underdog facing seemingly impossible odds. "I just would get so pissed. I've never been so pissed. I don't even know if they showed it, but I would throw things at the people who [voted] me in and I'm like, 'Bring it on. You're next,'" Emily says. "People really wanted to get rid of us, and we just wouldn't let them. There was a fierceness that came out that I didn't even know I had, and I loved it."

While she and Ty survived three eliminations together, her passion wasn't enough to carry both of them to a *Challenge* championship. "It was a really hard final, and Ty almost gave up, like, six times," she says. "I was dragging him up the mountain, like, 'No, we have to finish.'" And they did—but in third place. And while Emily was disappointed that she didn't win, she's grateful that Ty at least finished and didn't give up. She's also thankful that she got to spend that time before, during, and after the final in Iceland with Diem Brown (who passed away in 2014), which she says she'll treasure forever.

There were a lot of moments from that season that Emily remembers fondly and with pride, but it also featured her lowest *Challenge* moment of all time, one that led to a really dark but ultimately enlightening life lesson. After a night of partying, Emily and Camila Nakagawa thought it would be a funny prank to dress up as Ty and Paula, who had struck up a showmance that season. But things crossed a line when Emily smeared Nutella on her face to portray her partner. Since Ty is Black, the rest of the players still awake were shocked that she did blackface, but Emily was ignorant of the fact that what she had done was offensive. "I didn't understand what I was doing, and I so badly wish I did understand in the moment," she says. "I didn't even realize what it was until Diem woke up the next day, because nobody would talk to me about it that night. It was like, 'What did I just do? Everyone's quiet and angry, and nobody's telling me what happened.' Finally Diem woke up and said, 'What happened?' I said, 'I put Nutella on my face,' and as soon as I saw her face, I wanted to puke because I knew that I had done something so horrific that I was unaware of."

Ty threatened to leave the game until Emily tearfully apologized and they made up. But she says the issue didn't just end there for her. "I took full accountability for it and responsibility for it, because I absolutely should have known better and should have understood what I was doing," she says. "But it was hard; it took a long time for me to feel as if I could have any sort of conversation about race or any sort of conversation about being a part of change, because I felt like I was a part of the problem. I felt complete remorse and guilt for participating in something that was so much bigger than me and so important to address. I was oblivious and ignorant to the race issues that still existed, just completely naïve. I wanted so badly to be able to take back what I had done, but it happened, and I wanted to make it right."

Emily says it took a long time and a lot of apologies, hard conversations, and educating herself on what she had been sheltered from all her life. "I understood how much I needed to learn and go back to school and read books that cover all the types of history that we don't learn in school, especially in Missouri—and all over the country, unfortunately—to really dig into the history of what somebody who is not white has had to go through and recognizing how I can be a part of that change in everything that I do. How can I support that in my businesses, with my dollar; what can I do to give back? And I still have those conversations a lot, and I just ask for forgiveness but also make sure I practice what I preach. So many times where this happens, it's like, 'I don't want to be racist, I don't want to feel bad,' but that's white fragility. I needed to own that I did this and understand I was an active participant. It helped me understand how little I knew and how much I needed to get out of my white privilege world. And there's still so much more to do."

After her first two seasons, with all the high highs and low lows, Emily's life had completely changed. She was in the best physical shape she'd ever been in, she knew how to treat and fuel her body the right way, and she found the competitor inside of herself that she never knew existed, all while learning an important lesson along the way. But she also now understood she couldn't win *The Challenge* unless whomever she was paired with wanted it as badly as she did (if she wasn't lucky enough to be cast on a solo season). "It all depends on your partner; nothing mattered unless your partner was in it one hundred percent, and you can't want it for your partner like with Ty," she says. When she returned for *Rivals II* in 2013, the *Challenge* gods finally gave her a partner who wanted it as badly as she did. "To know that my partner was Paula, knowing how Paula is and how she has that switch that goes off in her head, it was amazing. She was so determined to make me proud and didn't want to let me down. And she wanted to make sure that I got to the final and that we won, and I felt that from her from the first second they said we were partners."

Everything Emily had been working toward led to this season, and while she knew she had her work cut out for her in keeping Paula calm, she also knew they couldn't be beat when it came to daily challenges. "We just kept winning and proving it to ourselves that we had everything we needed to win the whole thing," she says. They won six out of the ten challenges and never saw a single elimination that season before making the final. "It gave us the confidence we needed. If we doubted at all that we could do this, we now knew we could do it."

Emily also got a confidence boost from an unlikely source, minutes before the final began. "I have this sign that my mom shows up in ladybugs, and we were on a boat in Thailand about to launch this final and a ladybug landed on me," she says. "It was my good omen where I got this huge feeling of, 'I'm so in the right place.' It happened on *Champs vs. Stars*, too, during the final, which I also won."

But the *Rivals II* final wasn't a sure thing for Emily and Paula. After the first day, Cara Maria Sorbello and Heather Cooke were in first place, and while Emily and Paula avoided getting cut from the competition by beating Camila and Jemmye Carroll in the first leg, they knew they had to pick it up on the second day. "We were behind for a lot of that first part of the final, and Cooke and Cara Maria are athletes. They are no joke," Emily says. "It came down to the food checkpoint. We just had to eat faster, but it was disgusting. There was so much puking. We came in late, everyone else was already eating, so it was game time. We'll do whatever it takes, we'll eat whatever. And that's when we started to get momentum and catch up." Thanks to Paula housing plate after plate of chilies, pickled fish soup, worms, crickets, maggots, durian, and dried squid like it was Sunday brunch, they finally pulled into the lead, and they never let up for the rest of the final. "It took the last lap for it to really hit that we were going to win, because you just never know until it happens. When we finally got on the boat and realized we just won, it was so surreal."

Competing on *The Challenge* had already forever changed Emily's life in so many positive ways, but finally getting her first win gave her the confidence to take what she had learned about nutrition, fitness, and self-empowerment and help others go through the same health transformation she did. She now works as a nutritional therapy practitioner and self-help coach to inspire others to take their lives into their own hands. "Winning *The Challenge* was ultimately the blueprint for me in opening up my gym and all the online support that I have been able to provide through programs," she says. "And it just helped me build a platform to teach people about how to become their best selves."

All the good that Emily has been able to pass on to others never would have happened if she hadn't taken that chance and gone on *The Real World* despite not knowing anything about it. "I'm so proud of little Emily—she just showed up, terrified, didn't even know what MTV was, but she just kept showing up. And that's become a theme of my life," she says. "It's important for all of us to remember we just have to keep showing up—nothing happens if you don't show up and try to put yourself out there. Keep climbing the mountain and you'll be surprised at what you can accomplish."

And there are always more mountains to climb on *The Challenge*, which is why, after a four-year break, she's not ruling out a return to the franchise in the future. "Maybe I will do another one," she says. "I would be down. The feelers are out. I think it might be time."

HUNTER BARFIELD

Champion: *Final Reckoning*

Hunter Barfield wants to make one thing very clear: he *is* a *Challenge* champion—it's a fact. Still, many people don't actually consider him to be a true winner, since his *Final Reckoning* partner, Ashley Mitchell, took his half of the million-dollar prize money after they won the season together. "I know this is a book about *Challenge* champions and their stories, but I feel like people put an asterisk by my name because I didn't get any money," Hunter says. "That's always what bothered me more than her taking the money." That betrayal haunts him because Hunter went through hell and back to become a champ—physically, mentally, and emotionally—and when he finally won, becoming the first (and so far, only) *Are You the One?* alum to win *The Challenge*, he thought the eventual reward would make it all worth it. But he didn't get the prize he expected in more ways than just financial, and his journey to get there was much darker and more difficult than most. Fair warning: this isn't a story filled with the usual triumphs and happiness you'd expect from a *Challenge* champ. And yet it's no less meaningful, because Hunter refuses to let all the negative experiences define him, as a competitor or as a person. It's taken him a long time to get here, but he's more determined than ever to continue to learn and grow from each one.

When Hunter got his start on reality TV, he was no stranger to heartbreak. He'd just dropped out of college in his junior year because his girlfriend was pregnant, and he quit sports and rearranged his entire life in preparation to become a father. "We wound up losing the baby, and she left," he says. "I didn't go back to school, didn't go back to baseball. I was pretty traumatized, and I wanted something different. I thought, maybe the TV matchmakers will help me find my special person." He didn't find love on season three of MTV's experimental dating show in 2015, but it did open the door to an exciting new path for him on *The Challenge* instead.

"Everything happens for a reason. When I went on *Are You the One?*, I had no idea they were going to take people for *The Challenge*," he says. "I'm an extremely competitive person. I played college baseball, and football, baseball, and soccer my whole life, so this worked out even better than I could have imagined." When he got the call to join the cast for *Invasion of the Champions* in 2017, he admits he came in too arrogant and cocky. "I knew my athletic background gave me the advantage over other competitors. I wanted to play the game physically better than everyone on the show and just let that speak for itself." He quickly learned, however, that he couldn't ignore the political and social aspects of the game, no matter how hard he tried. "I was floored at how nasty things got so quick and how people turn on each other with lies and drama."

His rookie season was centered around the massive twist where, at the beginning, the players were told there were no *Challenge* champs in the cast. Halfway through the season, eight of the most legendary winners invaded the game, and now the Underdogs had to compete against them as well as each other. Hunter wasn't fazed by the influx of intense competition like his teammates were; he actually was even more excited to prove he had what it takes to win in light of the new twist. "It kicked me into another gear," he says. "Now, to be the best, I had to beat the best: the all-time greats. I can really make my mark on the show. Now is when the game really starts."

The first challenge in which the Underdogs competed against the Champions gave Hunter the opportunity to see if he measured up to the best, and he seized it. "Everybody had talked about Johnny Bananas, Johnny Bananas, Johnny Bananas. I knew that he was the GOAT, and he was the one that I looked up to on *The Challenge*." In an intense game of tackle football, Hunter set his sights on Johnny. "When the rocket launched the ball, I had no intention of going to get the ball whatsoever. I wanted to get my hands on Johnny Bananas. I grabbed him, I threw him down and rubbed his head in the dirt. I was just holding him down, and there was absolutely nothing he could do to get up. It was a big moment where I realized I can do this; I went against a giant and held my own. To see that I was actually overwhelming him, it juiced me up."

Hunter eventually met his match when he went up against his true enemy: puzzles. He was purged in a sudoku challenge right before the final. It was an eye-opening moment that taught him how important puzzle skills are on *The Challenge*, but at least he now knew what he needed to work on for future seasons (in addition to improving his cardio). "I also learned that my political game was extremely weak," he adds. "I'd seen it with my own eyes, and it was kind of alarming—people will do and say anything to win, and that was not how I played."

After *Invasion of the Champions* (where he placed in the top six), Hunter changed up his training to include more running and practicing puzzles. He was aware he needed to tone his arrogance down to be a better social player, and that meant altering his "all or nothing, win or bust" mentality. By the time he returned for *XXX: Dirty 30* a few months later, he felt physically and mentally the most prepared he's ever been for any season of *The Challenge,* past and future. "I put my heart and soul into that season," he says. Despite his personal mantra of playing with integrity, he wasn't even bothered by the fact that the season's theme was centered around casting the dirtiest, most unpredictable players the franchise had ever seen, because he formed an alliance with people he trusted implicitly: Cory Wharton and Nelson Thomas. The trio nicknamed themselves "Team Young Buck" as the new blood coming for the older, established champs. Their alliance put a massive target on their backs immediately, however, when Cory announced their intentions of taking out the top players. The rest of the house went after Team Young Buck ruthlessly as a result, forcing Hunter to compete in multiple, emotional eliminations against Cory and Nelson. He won against Cory but lost to Nelson, and then eventually beat Cory again in a Redemption House elimination to get back in the game.

"Nobody wanted to see me in the game, and they made us pick each other off," he says. "I did not know that I was going to have to go against my friends nonstop, and emotionally, that took a toll on me. We had love for each other as brothers, and typically, when I'm going into elimination against someone, it's cutthroat. I'm trying to tear you apart. I want to embarrass you to make sure you never want to compete against me again, and I did not have that feeling with Cory and Nelson. It's a lose-

Hunter knows how dirty the game can get.

lose. The other competitors don't want to celebrate with you, and I'm losing someone I trust." But he doesn't think making Team Young Buck's intentions known at the beginning of the season was a mistake, regardless of how it put a target on their backs. His only regret was not winning more daily challenges that season to keep himself safe, especially since his game ultimately ended because of an injury he got during an elimination against Leroy Garrett near the end of the season.

In a twist on Hall Brawl, Hunter and Leroy had to run through a wall of plastic wrap and around each other, and Hunter ended up smashing his hand during the first round's collision. "Essentially, I shattered my wrist, and I knew it wasn't going to be the same the rest of the season. Mentally, it was the last straw. I had been through hell that entire season, and I had persevered through it all. My girlfriend that I was planning on getting engaged to broke up with me over the phone.

My great-grandfather died while I was gone. I eliminated my friends. And this is how it ends?"

Even in as much pain as he was, Hunter still won that elimination against Leroy, but now he was competing with a full cast on his hand. He was allowed to remain in the game despite his injury, but he knew he was in trouble. "I was in major pain, but I couldn't let it be the end," he says. "I might not be able to win because, I mean, let's face it, I was numb from my elbow to the end of my fingers." But Hunter thought if Jordan Wiseley, who was born with only one hand and was also competing that season, could do well on *The Challenge*, then so could he. And if he could at least beat Jordan, who had been gunning for him all season, it would all be worth it. "I wanted to send him home because he'd tried everything he could at this point to send me home." He got his chance when he won the very next daily challenge and sent Jordan straight to the Redemption House. "I got my revenge. And if it wasn't for Nelson getting in that fight with Derrick [Kosinski], two people wouldn't have come back from the Redemption House. It's only because Nelson had to go home because of the altercation that Jordan got to come back in the game."

Eventually Hunter's injury proved to be an impossible obstacle to overcome when he was unable to complete the last daily challenge and got purged right before the final. And even though Jordan ended up winning that season, Hunter is proud that he previously beat Jordan and Jordan was only allowed to reenter the game through a technicality. It's the small but meaningful consolation prize for how broken Hunter felt when he got home. "That was supposed to be my season," he says. "I feel like I would have stamped my name as one of the *Challenge* greats if I could have capped that season off with winning. It really hit me after, like, you almost played a flawless game exactly like you wanted to. I was right there at the brink of a final but wasn't able to pull it off. I was pretty distraught because I had been through so much."

Hunter was immediately invited back the next season, *Vendettas* in 2018, to compete as a Mercenary in one elimination, but he was forced to say no. "I was extremely grateful that they even took the time to call me, but I had just gone through a six-hour surgery on my wrist," he says. "I was going to physical therapy five times a week, and there was no way that I could show up even as a Mercenary and potentially further damage it." At that point, his wrist was only at 65 percent mobility, and he was still in a lot of pain. "I was in a dark place, on heavy painkillers for the first time in my life, and I just really wasn't myself. I wasn't ready." He was devastated that he had to reject the invitation, but it turned out to be a blessing in disguise—he found out after the fact that, if he had said yes, he would have ended up competing against Nelson *again*. And that would have destroyed him. "I'm so glad I didn't do that because I love Nelson to death, but there's no way I could've thrown it. That's not who I am. I would've given it everything I had, and I don't know how I would've felt after if I would've won and took him out of the game. I think it all worked out."

When the next season, *Final Reckoning*, rolled around later that year, Hunter was finally ready to compete again after a long, difficult recovery process. "It took a long time for me to get back to even remotely close to physically what I was before, and I wasn't at my peak or anywhere near," he says. "I was told that I needed to have another surgery on my wrist. I never did it. I just could not put myself through that again. My wrist won't ever be the same, but I don't care. I trained my ass off because this was going to be my revenge season. The time is now. Put me in, Coach, I'm ready." He'd initially been informed that he was on the cast, but then he got switched to be an alternate instead. "I had given this show my everything, and I felt I deserved another opportunity. I'd shattered my wrist, I continued to compete, I still sent someone home, and I never quit. What more can I do? Then shortly after that, the producers were like, 'We still have plans for you, just stay on hold.'"

Hunter's prayers were finally answered when the producers decided that he'd get to be a Mercenary after all—with a twist. He and Ashley Mitchell entered the game a third of the way through the season as a pair to compete against rookies Angela Babicz and Faith Stowers in an elimination for the chance to steal their spot in the game. With everything Hunter had experienced so far on *The Challenge* to get to this point, he was back in his "all or nothing" mindset. "It was win or go home," he remembers thinking. "You have the opportunity you've been wanting. I'm used to my back being against the wall, so pin me back against the wall again and I'm coming out swinging. Hell will freeze over before I lose—there's no way. I had a mental edge I'd never experienced before in my life, because I wanted this more than anything I've ever wanted. I smelled blood in the water."

Hunter and Ashley won that elimination and officially entered the competition. Despite the "ups and downs" he'd experienced with Ashley during *Invasion of the Champions*—they'd hooked up and had a volatile relationship—he knew she was a good competitor who excelled at puzzles and social manipulation, which were his biggest weaknesses. He thought they'd make the perfect team. "There's not an elimination we can't win together," he says. "I thought I could trust her." But their partnership was toxic from the start, when Ashley hooked up with another player the first night they arrived at the house and Hunter proceeded to slut-shame her for it. They fought with each other throughout the rest of the season, and Hunter was caught on camera telling a group of players, "All I'm saying is, if this stupid fucking slut is gonna cost me a half a million dollars, then I'm coming for her family."

It all came to a head after they eventually won the final. Ashley was given the opportunity to steal Hunter's share of the prize money, since she finished with a slightly faster individual time. She stepped forward and declared, "This guy's belittled me, put me down, slut-shamed me, and also threatened my life and my family's life. I'm keeping the money." Hunter denied saying it in the moment, but the footage doesn't lie, and Ashley walked away with the entire million-dollar check for herself with no regrets in a move reminiscent of when Johnny decided to "take the money and run" after winning *Rivals III* with Sarah Rice two years prior.

Hunter believes that Ashley planned that betrayal from the start, and she's since admitted that's true because of how he'd treated her all season. "People don't know that at the start, she wrote it down in this little diary, 'We are in there as a team, but, Ashley, you are the final winner,' or whatever," Hunter says. "It was premeditated. I regret some of the things I said, absolutely, one million percent. This whole, 'You threatened her family,' I was in an emotional moment and I said something heated that I did not and would never in a million years follow through with. It's not what I meant, but I have to live and learn from the things I said. It was hell being partners with her. It was miserable, but in the end, we won together, and I would never have taken the money from her."

The betrayal stung even more because, at the very beginning of the final, Hunter had a massive fall while climbing down a ladder from a helicopter and injured his back. "I could have gone home right then, and Ashley would not have gotten any money at all," he says. "But I stayed for us." And during a pivotal eating portion, Hunter took charge and won their team the lead they needed to come out on top in the end. "I literally could have won by myself. Ashley contributed absolutely nothing. If it was not for the eating portion, Ashley and I do not win that final."

Losing half a million dollars was a massive blow for Hunter, but he cares more about the fact that he believes Ashley marred his hard-earned reputation of being a *Challenge* champion. "I know this is also hard for people to believe, but it was never about the money for me," he says. "It's the crown; it's the title. I just wanted to relish in that moment because, after everything I'd gone through, I finally did it. I didn't even really feel like I earned it that season, because I didn't win enough dailies or eliminations, but then I started thinking about it. All the other shit that I've been put through, all the other eliminations, the mental and emotional damage that I've experienced, ultimately, that's how I earned it. I want people to remember me as a *Challenge* champion for everything I'd accomplished and winning in only my third season."

But the best moment of his life immediately turned into the worst. "All the elation I felt was immediately gone," he says. "It's more so because, for the fans, it's like, 'You left with the exact same amount of money as all the losers. You're not a champion. She's the only champion.' I was just numb." Despite finally achieving the goal he'd worked so hard for, when Hunter got home, he was struggling more than ever. "Psychologically and emotionally, I didn't trust anybody after that. It changed me as a person. I was back in a really dark place." He says the experience triggered him to relive trauma from his childhood and his relationship with his mother. "A lot of people don't know this—my mother's a drug addict. She's never kept her word, was never really a mother, and when she left, my trust was already down from that. When Ashley took the money, that was my partner, another person I'm supposed to be close with. My trust was completely shot."

Hunter also realized he'd lost his inner passion for competition, which was something that had always defined him. "I didn't feel the same anymore, because it was the single most important thing that I won in my entire life, and I have nothing to show for it," he says. "It's tainted. My drive isn't what it once was. But I wanted revenge more than anything. And I wanted to win money so I'd shut anybody up who didn't consider me a *Challenge* champion. Now it became about the money, because that's the only way to erase the asterisk I have above my name."

Since winning *Final Reckoning*, Hunter hasn't been able to erase that asterisk. He returned one more time for the next season, 2019's *War of the Worlds*, and finished in sixth place after losing an elimination against "Ninja" Natalie Duran during the grueling final. "I gave it everything I had, and it wasn't enough," he says. "It just wasn't my final. Production had to give us IVs earlier than they planned because I physically couldn't stand up. I pushed my body past its physical limits. There was nothing more I could do, so I have no regrets."

It was all worth it in the end, though, because he did get his revenge on Ashley. Earlier that season, he and his partner, Georgia Harrison, were chosen to go into the first elimination, and he took the opportunity to pick Ashley and her partner, Chase McNary, as their opponents for a variation on Balls In. Ashley won the first point against Georgia, but then Hunter and Georgia won the next two rounds, sending Ashley and Chase home.

"It definitely brought some of the fire back for sure," he says. "I felt selfish for wanting to call them out, because this was Georgia's first season, and she was scared to death. But there was not a doubt in my mind that was the route I was going to go. And when I sent them home, it was like a weight was lifted off of me. It didn't give me the money back, but it was a good feeling because in that moment, I realized that no one can take away my drive for competing. That's who I am, no matter what."

It's been a long, difficult road, but Hunter's finally gotten to a place where he views every moment from his *Challenge* career as a positive learning experience. "It's made me mentally a stronger person," he says. "Anything that I go through now in my everyday life, I can equate it to what I've been through on *The Challenge*: 'You've been through worse before. You can get through this now.' And honestly, things don't get to me as much anymore. I don't get as stressed. I feel like I'm more level-headed and I've grown up. I've become a better person." It was the perfect preparation he needed for the next stage of his life, when he became a father a few months after *War of the Worlds* aired. "Now I have a son, and I actually have a little girl on the way. I'm a better dad for my kids because of everything. I'm more patient now. I'm less edgy. I'm a little bit less competitive now. But do not get it twisted: I want to come back and win so I can set up my kids for their future with the money. Now the drive to win isn't for me anymore—it's for them."

Hunter reveals he's already been invited back, but he had to say no because his daughter's due date conflicted with filming. He's hopeful he'll get another chance soon, though, to show how much he's changed and grown in his time away. "I have a whole different purpose for playing the game now," he says. "The fire is burning inside me brighter than ever."

THE TWO-TIME CHAMPS

YES DUFFY

Champion: *Challenge 2000*, *All Stars*

Breaking the rules usually gets players sent home from *The Challenge*. But for Yes Duffy, breaking a rule actually led to his biggest win. The *Road Rules: Semester at Sea* alum didn't cheat in a challenge. He didn't sneak out of the house, get into a physical fight, or do anything seriously wrong like that. The rule he broke? Sneaking an empty journal—an item prohibited by production—into the house on *All Stars* so he could write down his thoughts about how to succeed in the game. And it was his daily introspective writing that turned out to be the tool he needed to win his second *Challenge* championship after a twenty-year break from the show.

Yes walked into *All Stars* as a champion, having won his first season, *Challenge 2000*. But it was a much different experience back then. It was only the third season of *The Challenge*, and it was played in two teams of six: *Road Rules* alums versus *The Real World* alums. The format was more similar to a season of *Road Rules* than a modern-day *Challenge*, and Yes thinks that's why his *Road Rules* team demolished the *Real World* team. "We were doing things that we were already good at—the missions, driving across the country, doing ridiculous things—and it was an extension of the adventure that we already began," he says. "We kicked their asses. We learned real quick that Road Rulers got this shit down. The people that thrive on *The Challenge* even still today are the people who are calm and welcoming to the uncertainty of it, and Road Rulers, that was the name of the game for us. We'll jump into anything, any situation you want to throw at us."

One of Yes's favorite moments from his first winning season was setting the world record for bungee jumping . . . only to have it broken fifteen minutes later by Kat Ogden from the *Real World* team. "Kat beat me, and they don't even show it on the show that I got it for fifteen minutes first, but I remember!" he says. "We did all kinds of crazy, stupid stuff that season. We did demolition derbies. We jumped out of planes. We wrestled pigs. I loved every moment of it."

The prize money back then was nowhere near what winners make on *The Challenge* these days—Yes walked away with $11,254 for *Challenge 2000*—but for him, the real prize was the people he met and the experiences he had all season long. "We went to a lot of small communities around the United States, and that was very eye-opening as a young person to be traveling and just being welcomed into places so different from what I knew," he says. Growing up, Yes was inspired to become an activist by watching his mother fight for laborers' and sex workers' rights, and traveling on *Challenge 2000* amplified that drive to help others. "It gave me this opportunity to see how America has its own level of poverty and struggle, and it exploded my passions for recognizing the privilege we all have and actually wanting to do some greater good. It gave me a bigger purpose and a reason."

His next two seasons of *The Challenge* did not leave as big of an impact on him. When Yes returned for 2002's *Battle of the Seasons*, he was sent home first (making him the first man ever to be eliminated from a season of *The Challenge*), along with his fellow *Road Rules* alum Veronica Portillo (making her the first woman to be eliminated). He returned for *Battle of the Sexes* immediately after, and he made it about a third of the way through the season before getting eliminated. Yes thought his reality TV career would end there. He turned his focus to his career as an architect. He got married, had kids, and put *The Challenge* behind him. He didn't watch the show or keep up with it online (he didn't even know *The Challenge* was still airing new seasons).

So when he was invited to return twenty years later for the first season of the *All Stars* spin-off, he had no idea what to expect. A quick Internet search opened his eyes to exactly what he signed up for, and he started to have doubts. "I was like, 'Oh my God, I've got to be stronger. I've got to be a smart player. I've got to be a survivor. I've got to have allies.' But I felt I didn't have those strengths," he says. "I don't have social ties with the group. I knew I had to make friends fast, and it's not in my nature to do that." Before he left for Argentina, his wife gave him crucial advice. "She was like, 'Usually it takes weeks for people to get to know you, so you better speed up and get to know people right away. Don't be shy, say what's on your mind, and just be active.' You don't see it much on the show, but I was extremely active the whole time getting to know people, helping people, and carving my identity within the group. It was the most exhausting, difficult month of my life. Some people call it sitting in the background or skating by, but for me, it felt like work the whole time."

Because Yes hadn't stayed in the *Challenge* world, he was starting the season with a clean slate compared to the rest of the cast. And while he initially saw that as a disadvantage, he soon realized it was actually the opposite. "I didn't have a bunch of YouTube compilation videos about my wins and losses," he says. "What turned into an unforeseen strength was that I started to play up the fact that I don't know much about anybody and I don't know much about the game. I was just brutally honest and trusting. I showed up with no weapons, no assumptions, no strategy other than to open my mind and heart to understand people and make some friends. And I was like, 'Holy shit, this is working.'"

Yes knew going in with the strategy of being fully honest might be a tougher path to take in a game where people are known for lying and backstabbing, but he never considered doing anything else. "I had a lot on the line because my kids are going to watch it, which was the biggest motivator," he says. "And other kids are going to watch it also, so I had to get it right. Don't lie, don't bullshit. You couldn't pay me a million dollars to lie to somebody on television. It's just not worth it. And every day, it was working. I'm trusting everybody and they're trusting me. I'm not gunning for anybody. I'm just listening and learning and respecting everyone and that helped to build this great community, even in a place where we compete every other day."

That positive, open, and friendly attitude saved him when he was almost voted into the final elimination of the season. It was his impassioned speech about how hard he worked to make new friends and didn't rely on old alliances that swayed Aneesa Ferreira to vote Nehemiah Clark instead of him. Now that Yes was guaranteed a spot in his first-ever final, he was equal parts excited and terrified. "I panicked, but I also welcomed the panic," he says. "I was ready to win because every single day, I wrote about winning. I imagined winning. I didn't let doubt kick in, ever. I'd never let the thought of possibly losing even come into my mind, which is unusual for me because normally, I'll analyze it every different way."

And this is where his contraband journal came in. He hid the forbidden notebook under his pillow, and every day he would take time to quickly write down a new thought about how to succeed—both in the game and in life—and study it in secret, because production had banned any writing materials in an effort to get the players to focus on each other rather than on an individual activity like writing or reading. "It's called 'A Journal on Winning,' and I just wrote one sentence at a time, just little nuggets of things I want to try in life and also that will help me win," he says. "The first one is, 'Be authentic.' Another is, 'Don't play the game, change the game.' 'I often only try what I believe is possible but I came here to achieve the impossible.'" Some days his thoughts were literal, like "Only take what you're gonna eat," and other days they were more inspirational, like "There is always more in the tank."

"They were tools for survival," Yes says. "And if you survive long enough, you win. That was my mindset. You do so much thinking there, and it was great to see what bubbles to the top of the anxious thinking. 'If you think about losing, you have already lost.' It was this secret strength where I would whisk away a nugget of positive productive thoughts, and it was a form of focus in a place and at a time where there was no focus. It was powerful. We give a lot of attention to the nervous-making, anxiety-inducing things, the problems that we have—that's just in our nature. To give real attention to the things that are fucking awesome takes effort, and that's how I survived on *The Challenge*. It was how I started each day: feeling inspired rather than terrified about what T.J. was going to throw at us tomorrow."

When Yes reads back through his journal now, he still fully believes in every single thought he wrote down. "Whether I live by it is a different story, but that's the challenge ahead of all of us," he says. "But they are pure thoughts that I want to live by, and that's really what *The Challenge* was for me. I was trying to be who I want to be, not just who I am. It was an aspirational thing for me when I went on *The Challenge* to try to be really trusting of people and open-minded. That was the social challenge for me, and it worked out."

Yes is proud of how he was able to adapt in the game and take his weaknesses and turn them into strengths. "It's one of the best things I've done in my life. That journey was really uplifting and empowering. It changed my life," he says. "I feel stronger than I've ever been. I'm more fit than I've ever been, thanks to *The Challenge*." He was inspired by watching his *All Stars* castmates Darrell Taylor, Mark Long, and Derrick Kosinski working out throughout the season. As a result, when he got home, he decided to overhaul his lifestyle into one that's much healthier. "I've really enjoyed hanging out with these people who have invested in their fitness throughout their twenties and thirties, and now there's no going back to being unhealthy, overeating, and not taking care of my body."

But perhaps the most important change that came about thanks to his *All Stars* win was to his mental health. The season was filmed in early 2021 and, like everyone, Yes was a year into the COVID-19 pandemic. "We were all beat up and hurting then," he says. "And when I came back, I just felt hopeful again. I felt thankful. I felt privileged. I felt powerful. And I'm so inspired to just do more."

JODI WEATHERTON

Champion: *The Gauntlet 2, The Duel*

In a game as unpredictable as *The Challenge*, it's rare to find a player who's as reliably good as Jodi Weatherton. It doesn't matter if it's 2005 or 2021—you want her on your team. The *Road Rules: X-Treme* alum competed on only four seasons, and yet she's a two-time champion and has won more daily challenges than most competitors who have been on twice the amount of seasons. While she's not perfect—puzzles will always be her biggest weakness—she's one of the best competitors to have ever played the game.

Growing up, Jodi never felt like she was the best at anything. She had a decent athletic background as a kid, playing all kinds of team sports like basketball, volleyball, and softball, and doing outdoor activities like waterskiing, riding dirt bikes, and Rollerblading. She was always strong physically, but she never found the one thing she was truly great at. "I know how to do a lot of different things, but it's like I was a jack-of-all-trades, master of none," she says. And because she moved around a lot as a kid, she also didn't have many close friends. "I was always the new kid and there's a lack of assurance in that. Those connections were harder and harder for me to make."

By the time she made her *Challenge* debut on *The Inferno II*, she knew her physically strong exterior didn't match how she felt on the inside. "I wish I had more self-confidence before I went on *The Challenge*," she says. "I don't think I really knew who I was as a person. I wish I could go back and tell myself, 'Be sure of yourself, because you are cool,' but I just don't think I believed in myself in that way."

Her first season of *The Challenge* didn't do much to change that, either. Jodi admits that she didn't really know what she was getting herself into on *The Inferno II* because she had never watched a season before showing up. "It was definitely like I was thrown to the wolves as the new rookie," she says. "I had no awareness of what to do. I was just like, 'We're all here to have fun, and it's going to be so great.' I was very, very wrong." Jodi overestimated how much her *Road Rules* castmate Derrick Kosinski would be able to guide her that season, especially since they were on opposite teams. "I didn't realize that he really had no control over anything on his team. He couldn't really help me as much as I was thinking." Without any real allies, she knew she was in trouble early on. "I learned that people are out for blood on these things and you have to be smart," she says. "It is about who you know and who you're friends with. I didn't know that everyone contacted people before the show started, making those connections before I got there. I went in with absolutely no plan."

When Jodi was picked to go into elimination, at least she went out swinging. She picked Veronica Portillo as her opponent even though everyone assumed she was going to pick Tonya Cooley. "She was a threat and a ringleader, so it would be smart to take her out if I could," Jodi remembers. "I could tell that Veronica was nervous to go in against me because she wasn't expecting it, and I was hopeful it was going to be something physical. But unfortunately for me, we just had to spin and wrap ourselves up in cloth. She had a ballet background, and I was dizzy as crap. I'm not good at that, apparently. I ended up looking like a big tool and went home." She was so upset after that loss that she never even finished watching the season. She still hasn't seen any of the episodes past her elimination. "This many years later, I cannot. I don't even know what they did in the final. I'm still mad I missed it."

When Jodi got home from *The Inferno II*, she did a lot of self-reflection on what went wrong in her rookie season. "I learned it's best to not go into elimination if you can avoid it, because that was some janky crap where it was anyone's game," she says. "My whole goal in every season after that is avoid elimination, because eliminations level the playing field. And to earn your safety from ridiculousness that could send you home and make you look stupid on national TV, you've got to be better physically or mentally or have a leg up over people in the actual challenges."

She now understood what she had to do to win when she returned for *The Gauntlet 2* on the Rookie team. "I definitely made contact with other castmates first and made all these connections before I got there," she says. "But I also knew I had to prove myself—I'm not just going to expect that my team is going to want me around if I'm sucking. My whole strategy became: I have to do well in every single challenge to the best of my ability, but also try to cultivate those friendships the best I can while I'm there so people not only want me around because I'm good, but they want me around because I'm fun to be around." She knew she needed to build the kind of relationships she had always wanted but never had from a young age, but it wasn't easy because now she was also fighting to change the narrative that she "is one of the more boring Challengers," which she says is the feedback she gets the most from fans. "Everyone was always like, 'Jodi is so boring,' and I'm really not! When people meet me they're usually like, 'Wow, you're surprisingly funny.' *Surprisingly* funny. Like I'm normally so dull? Gosh, that's tough to hear. I may not get involved in the drama so much, but I'm there to be me and make genuine connections with people."

With her wide-ranging sports and athletics background, she knew she could handle whatever was thrown at her during daily challenges, so she started to instead focus on finding the X factor that would put her team over the top. "I was trying to think of out-of-the-box things to help my team in each challenge," she says. "Like one time, there was this crossbar where the other team was sitting on it, and we just couldn't get anybody off. I came up with the strategy to help us win. I was like, 'Let's pull it opposite directions rather than what we've been doing,' and then Syrus [Yarbrough] fell off. Anytime you can do something like that, you have to take that chance."

As Jodi started earning the reputation for being a great competitor on her team, she noticed that it also helped her social game. "I feel lucky because *The Gauntlet 2*, the way it was set up, was so in my wheelhouse," she says. "I was a solid competitor, and if you're doing well and helping the team, they're not going to want to send you home. Me doing the best that I could and helping win some of the challenges, they wanted to keep me to help win the final." And while she was taking the competition as seriously as if it were her job, she also never let herself forget how much fun it all was. "I love the competition so much that I don't want to miss a single thing. I just want to be a part of all of it, because when else do you have the opportunity to do these crazy things they set up for us? Never. You can't even pay money to do some of these things."

By the time she got to her first final, she was excited to prove herself even further in a marathon-style race. Her team ended up winning, but she was disappointed in how the events actually unfolded. "[The producers] had something big set up for us to do for that final, and the rumor is that the guys on the Veteran team saw it, so production had to scramble and do something real quick to switch it up," she says. "We ended up doing some janky poker game where you had to bet your booty on these different games. We ended up winning just by eating burritos." Jodi laughs at how the Veteran team underestimated her and Ibis Nieves when it came to the burrito-eating competition. "We can *eat*. If you threw up, you were out. Jamie [Murray] was starting to feel sick, and Ibis said, 'Jamie, just stop eating. We've got this,' and Ibis and I ate it all." Jodi remembers feeling extremely nauseous by the end of it, but the eating portion put the Rookies so far ahead of the Veterans that they didn't even have to finish out the rest of the final. "I felt so sick, but I was so happy that I didn't eat all that gross burrito for nothing."

She didn't get the final experience she had been hoping for, but Jodi was now officially a *Challenge* champion. It was a major moment to celebrate, yet she still felt like something was missing in her life. That's why she decided to attend a yearlong program at a Bible school to recenter herself. "I had everything the world says that you need. I was living the life that everyone was jealous of, but I still didn't feel fulfilled," she says. "I grew up in a Christian home, and I really lost touch with what I believed. I didn't know what I felt anymore, and something was drawing me to go figure it out." During that time, she was invited to join the cast of *Fresh Meat*. "I remember really wanting to do it, but also knowing that I should stay and finish out that year I committed to in that school, so I said no to *Fresh Meat*. Thank goodness I did, because had I said yes, maybe I would not have been asked to be on *The Duel* and my life would have been totally different."

When Jodi finally stepped foot back into the *Challenge* world in Brazil for *The Duel*, she felt as if everything in her life had been preparing her for that moment. She now knew how to excel in the physical and social aspects of the game, and she felt mentally and emotionally stronger than ever thanks to her short hiatus from the show. "I don't know if I expected to win *The Duel*, but I want to win everything," she says. "That was my mindset going in. I got there, I looked around, sizing everyone up, seeing who else was there, and I was thinking, 'I think I could do it. I think I could beat all these people.' Then we found out it was a solo season and I was confident, but I was also cautious. I didn't want to let myself get too excited. But I was."

The Duel was the first season of *The Challenge* that would produce an individual male and female winner, and for the first time, Jodi wasn't pushing herself to win for teammates or anyone other than herself, which gave her a new kind of self-assurance she'd never felt before. Each daily challenge win was fulfilling in a new way because of that, and her confidence kept growing. By the end of the season, she and Svetlana Shusterman outlasted all the other women and faced off against each other in the final. "I will never forget when they flew us into the final in a helicopter," she says. "That was a once-in-a-lifetime moment, and at that point, I felt like I already won." The final didn't cater to all of Jodi's strengths—it began with a soccer kickoff, which is the only sport Jodi didn't play growing up, and there was also a giant puzzle that she initially thought Svetlana solved first—but she ended up winning definitively. "They want to make it look close on television, but I think I won by at least twenty minutes."

Crossing the finish line and becoming the first solo female winner of *The Challenge* (alongside Wes Bergmann, who won for the men) felt like the ultimate reward for all her personal growth and perseverance over the years. "I cried, and I mean, those were genuine emotions—disbelief, happiness, joy. I was in a euphoric state," she says. And walking away with the biggest prize money *The Challenge* had ever awarded (at that point) was the cherry on top. "I just thought, 'I feel good. I can be done with this now,'" she remembers. "I had been doing shows for four years; I got everything I could possibly get out of it. I think I'm ready to end on a high note and start my life. I'm ready to get a full-time job, get married, and have kids. And that's exactly what I did." Jodi met her husband and got married a year and a half after *The Duel*, and she calls walking away from *The Challenge* at that moment "the best decision I ever made."

"I never regretted it," she says. "We got pregnant pretty much right away, and then I was in that phase in my life where I was having babies. I really, genuinely thought I was never doing the show again because I had proved to myself everything that I felt I needed to, and I was really happy with where I'm at in my life." It was always her dream to be a stay-at-home mom, and while she loved getting to take care of her kids full-time, she often found herself unfairly comparing herself to other mothers who also had successful careers. Her husband encouraged her to find something she loved that she could do while still taking care of their kids, and because she always loved being active, she decided to try her hand at becoming a fitness instructor. "I didn't know if I actually was going to be good at this or not, but I had to take that step to find out," she says. "I went and got my certification and ended up loving it."

Looking back at the person she was before she started her *Challenge* journey, Jodi knows there's no way her younger self would have ever taken that leap to become an instructor of anything—especially since she actually failed the first program she applied to. "It's scary to be vulnerable and put yourself out there like that, knowing there's a chance you could fail," she says. "It took me a long time to get to that point where I didn't just go, 'This is not my thing,' and walk away. No, I rallied, I sent in another video, and got some of the highest marks you can get, and I ended up teaching group fitness classes for twelve years. Persevering even when things get hard is when you find the best stuff."

Jodi eventually returned to *The Challenge* in 2021 for *All Stars 2* for two reasons. She couldn't pass up the nostalgic "family reunion" experience, and she had just turned forty and wanted to see if she still had it in her to compete at a high level. "It felt like the timing was right in my life," she says. "My kids are old enough, they're not babies anymore. I was in between a part-time job and starting a full-time job."

Despite the fact that she hadn't competed on the show in over fifteen years, Jodi dominated the competition even more than she did when she was younger. She won almost every single daily challenge, won her first elimination against Sophia Pasquis, and was on track to do well in the final with her partner, Brad Fiorenza, potentially getting her third win . . . until they made a simple-yet-fatal mistake in a challenge that sent them into the final elimination of the season, in which they lost to Darrell Taylor and Janelle Casanave. "If I would have just taken a minute to breathe, or a minute to process things with my partner, maybe I could have not made those mistakes," she says. "I think the thing I need to work on now is forgiving myself and letting things go. Allow myself to feel all those deep things and then put it away and not think about it constantly, because that's not healthy."

Even though Jodi didn't get her third win on *All Stars 2*, she's still forever grateful for how *The Challenge* changed her life. The money she won from her early seasons allowed her to build and take care of the family she always wanted. And competing on the show, both then and now, helped her find the inner self-confidence to match her outer strength. That's why she isn't ruling out another return to the franchise in the future: "It just all comes down to timing."

M.J. GARRETT

Champion: *The Gauntlet 2, All Stars 2*

The odds of winning *The Challenge* are extremely low. In the first few seasons, the odds were fifty-fifty, since it was just *The Real World* teams competing against *Road Rules* alums. Season five, 2002's *Battle of the Seasons*, was the first time players were voted out of the game, and two seasons later on *The Gauntlet*, eliminations were introduced. The rest is history: winning *The Challenge* became more and more difficult with each new twist that raised the stakes and lowered the odds for competitors. But when M.J. Garrett arrived for his rookie season on *The Gauntlet 2* in 2005, that didn't matter to him. He expected to win because of his background as a college athlete. And he was right: he walked away as a champion that season. But his complete absence of doubt when he arrived for his first season of *The Challenge* is ironic, given that his extreme fear of failure has always been his biggest weakness. It took him a long time to get over that, but you wouldn't know it from his *Challenge* career.

After filming *The Real World: Philadelphia*, M.J. was having too much fun basking in his new MTV fame—getting paid for appearances and speaking at colleges—to even consider signing up for a new show. So when he was offered a spot in the *Inferno II* cast, he actually turned it down. "I was thinking that I wanted to take advantage of doing these appearances and stuff, and boy, did I regret that," M.J. says. "Because then, of course, I watched my buddy Landon [Lueck] on it, and he won. The next time they asked me to do it, for *The Gauntlet 2*, I was ready to go and compete."

At this point, M.J. was just a couple of years out of college at Vanderbilt University, where he had been playing football for the NCAA Southeastern Conference Division I team. "I had a good enough career to where I thought that I was going to be able to make it in the NFL, but it didn't work out for me," he says. When he didn't go on to become a professional football player, his biggest fear came true. "All of a sudden, I had this great education, a wonderful degree at a top school, but I'd always been a football player. I was really lost and didn't know what my next step was going to be. [That's why] *The Real World* was truly life-changing for me as a person. But *The Challenge* is more my bag, being an ex-athlete. It really fed that need to compete that I have."

Coming from such an intense sports background, M.J. didn't think he needed to prepare for his first season of *The Challenge*. "I was traveling nonstop doing appearances, so I literally rolled up to *The Challenge* without getting in the gym that much," he says. "I just really didn't think that *The Challenge* would be that hard because of what I had done on the collegiate level. I thought that they could put me in any situation and I would be okay because I was a natural athlete, but, oh baby, it's nothing like playing organized sports at all."

While M.J. is grateful that he had experience playing football, basketball, and baseball, he immediately learned in those first few days that *The Challenge* is a whole other game entirely. "In organized sports, you know exactly what you need to do to be successful. You've practiced those plays, you've practiced your position, and when you show up to the game, you already know who your competition's going to be," he says. Which was perfect for him, since he always pushed himself to be overly prepared on the field so he wouldn't fail. "But in *The Challenge*, you have no clue. You don't know when you show up if you're going to have to use your brain, your brawn, a partner, if it's going to be solo, if it's going to be a team. It doesn't matter how great of an athlete you are, if you can run a mile in five minutes and fifteen seconds, or even if you're not afraid of heights, you just never know what that day is going to bring you. And there is the pressure of having to go home. *The Challenge* is a true test of not only athleticism, but also the ability to conquer your nerves more than anything."

Underestimating *The Challenge* is usually a guaranteed ticket home, but M.J. got lucky as his team, the Rookies, beat the Veterans and he won his first season. "We had an amazing, amazing team. Alton [Williams] was our team captain from day one all the way through the final. I was just in the right place at the right time. I really didn't have to do much during *The Gauntlet 2*." M.J. laughs as he recalls how he, Landon, and Alton didn't even have to compete in the final, because their team had already won enough points that it would be impossible for the Veterans to catch up. "But I did learn a lot about the social game because I hadn't met any of these people before. I came in with no relationships at all, other than Landon because he was on *The Real World* with me. So I had to get in and develop relationships in a very quick amount of time not only on my team, but then also with the Veterans because I knew that I would probably do a show with them at another time."

It was just one way in which M.J. was already honing his political strategy by becoming a top social player. "I realized that relationships are just so important if you wanted to do more, and I never really viewed it that way when I was playing in college," he says. "Yeah, you wanted to be a good teammate, but it was different because once the game was over, it was over. But in *The Challenge*, when the competition ends, those relationships still affect the game."

With his first championship secured and a little extra cash in the bank thanks to his prize money, M.J.'s ego grew. "Winning my first season, I was like, 'God, I'm going to win every single *Challenge* that I'm on, this is easy,'" he says. "And then look, I didn't win another one for almost seventeen years."

It's not for lack of trying, however. M.J. was "bit by the *Challenge* bug" right away and was eager to compete again. But he wasn't invited back on the cast like he expected to be. "I have a very unique *Challenge* career because after winning *The Gauntlet 2*, I was brought in as an alternate for the next two seasons," he says. "Like on *Gauntlet III* one of the guys had to leave unexpectedly for a family emergency, they literally called me and said, 'Can we get you to Mexico tomorrow?' I showed up to compete after everybody had already met, after people had already put some groundwork in on the political side of things. And I was not in good shape at all. I did not make it very far."

The next time M.J. was invited back was for *The Duel II*, once again as a replacement after C.T. Tamburello and Adam King were kicked off for their brutal fight at the beginning of the season. "After the infamous C.T. and Adam fight, they brought me in to backfill for C.T.," M.J. says. "People were still shell-shocked. The room that I moved into, there were holes in the wall, the bed was broken, it looked like a war had gone on inside that house. They called me the night it happened because they knew that they were going to kick them off the show. And then I was on a plane the next day flying to New Zealand. They hadn't even had their first challenge yet."

Even though M.J. didn't miss any of the competition that season, he still felt like being a replacement put him at a huge disadvantage in the game. "I was never really prepared after my first season, because I was brought in as an alternate both times. And that really affects you, when you don't know that you're about to be competing—not just physically, but emotionally and mentally, too." He thinks that if he had been cast on *The Gauntlet III* and *The Duel II* as part of the original cast rather than as a replacement, his performance on those two seasons would have been drastically better. "Without a doubt. There's so much that goes on after the casting has happened. Everybody would start calling each other before you even met up on-site, so you had an idea who's going to be on the show and people would have some soft alliances going into the show. But whenever you're brought in as an alternate, you don't have that opportunity. You're way behind."

On *The Gauntlet III*, M.J. was thrown into an elimination pretty quickly after arriving late in the season. It was his first elimination ever, too, since he had avoided them in his first season, and he doesn't mince words about how it went: "It sucked." His opponent was Frank Roessler, and because M.J. was still riding high from his championship, he expected to win. "Frank was a decent athlete, but I didn't feel like he should've beat me," he says. "But he did. He put it to me. We were tied at the ankles doing reverse tug-of-war in the sand, and he just lay there and dug in while I used all my energy to try to pull him. I couldn't even budge him, and I was a lot bigger than him. He just waited for me to tire out and I had nothing left in the tank. I learned that you can't just go into eliminations and try to use brute strength—you have to have a strategy. You've got to find an edge."

Losing to Frank still haunts M.J. to this day—he was coming off winning his rookie season, he felt on top of the *Challenge* world, and then he got absolutely demolished right away when he returned. He didn't know how to handle failing. "That's the one that still sits with me. I don't have any closure with that," he says. "If I could go against Frank again right now, I freaking would. Anywhere, anytime, anyplace, it doesn't matter. I remember when I was being put in the vehicle to go back to the airport and fly out of Mexico, man, I was just . . . I was physically ill because I just knew that I'd left a lot on the table."

That's why M.J. hit the ground running when he arrived on *The Duel II*. Despite being a replacement again, he refused to let his game end as early as it did on *The Gauntlet III*. He knew he'd once again be targeted for coming into the competition late, so he got to work on the political side of the game and did everything he could to make connections and alliances as fast as possible. "I was fighting for my life," he says. "I was part of a great alliance with Mark [Long] and Evan [Starkman] and Landon and Brad [Fiorenza]. That season was when I learned how important your rooming situation is, because we were the last five guys there, and we all happened to be in the same room. I don't care what anybody says, where you lay your head at night is extremely important in the *Challenge* house. I was in a great alliance because of our room, but I knew that I was always toward the bottom of it, so I had a good feeling that I was going to have to compete quite a bit. It wasn't going to be a walk through to the final."

He was right. M.J. ended up in three eliminations that season and won his first two, against Ryan Kehoe and Dunbar Merrill. "But then Brad got the best of me," M.J. says. "Sometimes you get eliminations that just don't fit your skill set, and that one did not. We had to climb up a pole, and Brad is going to out-climb me every day of the week because I'm quite a bit bigger. But I was able to walk away from that one with the feeling that I competed as hard as I could, I played the game as well as I could, considering that I came in as an alternate, and I got beat by somebody who beat me fair and square. There's nothing I could've really done differently. And then my *Challenge* career went on pause until 2021."

By this point, M.J. had two young daughters and was focusing on his family and his career outside of reality TV. He remembers being considered for the cast of *The Island* in 2008, as well as a few other seasons of *The Challenge*, but he also understands why he ultimately wasn't chosen. "I was never really one of the more dramatic people on the show. And in my life, I was in a different place, so I took myself out of the pool in a lot of ways," he says. "They did call me several times, but I never made the final cut, and even if I would have, I don't know if I would've pulled the trigger on it."

It wasn't until his daughters convinced him to get on social media in early 2020 that he started thinking about *The Challenge* again. It was coincidentally right around the same time the #WeWantOGs campaign was in full force, but M.J. couldn't join the first season of *All Stars* due to scheduling: "When they

M.J. sizing up the *All Stars 2* competition before taking home another win.

were filming, I was in Costa Rica doing ayahuasca, this crazy, off-the-wall thing, for me, at least, doing some soul-searching and self-healing things." But he watched that first season and fell in love. "It was something I had to do, and that's when I reached back out to Mark and was like, 'Man, I would definitely love to be able to do the next one if you guys do another one,' and next thing I know, *boom*, I'm in Mexico."

Not being able to join the cast for the first season of *All Stars* turned out to be a blessing in disguise for M.J., since he knew he wasn't in the right shape, physically or mentally, to return to *The Challenge* and be successful after being away for so long. "Going into season two, I was definitely ready," he says. "I was training with a guy in Nashville who's an ex–special ops dude. He was focusing on training me not only on the physical side, but also the mental and the emotional side. He would do what he called 'taking you to the black,' where he would take me to a place where my body was totally exhausted, and then he would give me mental and problem-solving things to do when I was in that state. It was literally perfect for going into season two of *All Stars*, because that was next level."

Watching the first season of *All Stars* also gave M.J. a clue into just how much *The Challenge* had evolved since he was last on it. But experiencing how difficult the competition had become was still a major shock when he arrived. "It was hands down the hardest thing I've done in my life, physically, emotionally, and mentally," he says. Even though he came into *All Stars 2* feeling prepared, he was the most nervous he'd ever been, and it kicked his oldest insecurity into overdrive. "Something that has driven me since I was a child has been the fear of failure. People can handle that in different ways, but I've always been super concerned about not being successful or finishing last or not reaching my potential." He knows that can be a positive motivator for others, but it always manifested as negative feelings for him. "That is something that has always pushed me on *The Challenge*: I've never wanted to be embarrassed. I've never wanted to fail. Fear has always been a major driving force for me in these things."

But thanks to *All Stars 2*, he was finally able to bury that fear of failure—literally. "We did a really cool thing before the final started that they didn't air, before we got on those blocks for the overnight part," M.J. says. "One of the producers came up and said, 'I want you all to write down your greatest fears, and then we're going to bury them in the sand.' The word that I wrote down that night was 'fear.' I wanted to look at all of this stuff as an opportunity and have more of a positive spin on it rather than continue to be afraid of failing, so I buried that fear before that final started. And then I won. How crazy is that? That was a powerful moment for me because I took that moment very seriously."

Running the *All Stars 2* final with his partner, Jonna Mannion, also taught him that no matter how difficult or impossible things may seem, giving up is never an option. They finished the first phase of the final in dead last after Teck Holmes and Ayanna Mackins, who were behind them, quit. But in the second phase, M.J. and Jonna ended up winning the whole thing, earning M.J. his second *Challenge* championship. "I mean, especially with that final, you never really knew what was going to happen," he says. "You've just got to keep going, because if you're not winning at the beginning, you never know what can happen toward the middle or the end of these things."

Crossing the finish line with half a million dollars was one of the best moments of his life, but the reason M.J. calls *All Stars 2* life-changing has more to do with how he was finally able to overcome his fear of failure. In the past, that always held him back from taking risks, especially when it came to his career in the general contracting world. "After doing season two of *All Stars*, I'm taking the biggest risk ever: I'm starting a whole new career," he says. When he decided to do *All Stars 2*, he "had to make some career decisions because I was gone for so long for that show. I'm still picking up the pieces and trying to figure out what exactly I'm going to do and what it is that I truly want to do. There's something bigger out there for me and it's scary not knowing, but I don't really have the fear of failure like I did before."

Plus, M.J. is now more fired up to win *The Challenge* than ever before. "I'm very proud of my two *Challenge* wins. And hopefully, I'll have a third win," he says. "I want to keep racking them up. This has changed my life, because I had this feeling of despair not being able to compete anymore in football, the sport that I loved, and then being able to compete again in a different type of sport has been an honor. If that phone ever rings again, I'm going to say, 'Yes, sign me up.'"

RACHEL ROBINSON

Champion: *The Gauntlet, The Duel II*

Rachel Robinson will never forget the way it feels to win *The Challenge*. She's enjoyed that indescribably fulfilling moment twice in her career—first on *The Gauntlet* in 2003 and then six years later on *The Duel II*—and she wishes everyone else could experience it at least once in their lives. "Standing on the top of the hill, nobody can take that away from you," she says. "And I know that is ultimately what everybody wants, but I think people come at winning in such a stagnant way, like, 'I won because I'm the best,' or, 'I won because I'm the strongest.'" For Rachel, winning means so much more than the stereotypical or even literal definitions of the word. And while there's obviously no *figurative* way to win a *Challenge* championship, she explains that coming in first place isn't the most important part of competing for her. "I really do believe winning is showing up for yourself, making moves that nobody saw coming, putting yourself out there even if it's scary. That, to me, is a winner, even if it doesn't work out in the end."

She didn't always feel that way. Growing up, Rachel played every sport in the book and enjoyed finding new ways to challenge herself. "I'm a competitor at heart," she says. "I love the heart rate you get when you're about to do something that's crazy. But when I tore my knee my junior year of high school, it kind of redirected my life." Rachel had always thought she'd go on to play sports in college and maybe even professionally, but the way her coaches treated her after she got injured made her feel like she was replaceable. "I realized I didn't really want to play sports seriously after that. I'd rather be a normal college kid and valued for who I am, not what I do."

The "normal" chapter of her college experience didn't even last one full semester. On a whim, she auditioned at an open casting call for *The Real World* and *Road Rules* and got a callback right away. She was eighteen at the time, too young to be cast on *The Real World: Las Vegas*, so she ended up on *Road Rules: Campus Crawl* instead. As an out lesbian who had drive, talent, and presence, and who wasn't afraid to speak her mind about even the most controversial topics, she was a reality TV gold mine. After *Road Rules*, producers immediately invited her on *The Challenge*. "I was packing my bags to leave *Road Rules* and the producers pulled me aside and they said, 'Don't unpack, you're leaving in two weeks for *Battle of the Sexes*,'" Rachel remembers. "Then I would come home from a *Challenge* only to repack for another *Challenge*. They were like, 'Don't get too comfortable. You're leaving for *The Gauntlet*.' 'Don't get too comfortable, you're going to *Battle of the Sexes 2*.' I was loving it because I was hungry for new experiences."

She had no idea what to expect from her rookie season on *Battle of the Sexes*, but she certainly didn't predict that her own teammates would target her for being a strong, athletic competitor, since she thought that would be seen as an asset. "I didn't understand how it wasn't something that worked in my favor with the other women, like, 'Rachel's strong so we should keep her around for our team,'" she says. "It was like, 'Rachel's really strong, let's get rid of her.'" She was voted out early, and it opened her eyes to the fact that there was more happening within the game that affected her. "I was so upset, because I was having the time of my life in Jamaica, and I took it a little bit for granted. After that season, I learned that your position is never safe in the game and to expect the unexpected."

Rachel returned the next season for *The Gauntlet* with the intention of making sure no one cut her fun short again. That meant figuring out a strategy that kept her out of eliminations. Thankfully, the *Road Rules* team had their Gauntlet queen in Sarah Greyson, who won five eliminations that season, setting a record that still has never been broken for the most elimination wins in a single season (Wes Bergmann and Casey Cooper tied that record during *Fresh Meat*). "That's what I credit my first win to: staying out of eliminations," Rachel says. "The thing about Sarah is she enjoyed it, whether she wants to admit it or not. She would go in and come back super pumped. She felt very vindicated every time she went in and won, and she didn't really care about the challenges." Eventually Rachel made it to the final with her *Road Rules* team, and they won. "My first win came almost as a surprise. We had a very large team going into the final, and it was not in our favor. We were nine people competing against five—four of them very strong men and then Coral [Smith], who was very good. We just went into it saying, 'We're going to try our best,' and then before we knew it, we were in the lead, and then all of a sudden, we won."

Not giving up in the face of unfavorable odds made winning her first *Challenge* championship in only her second season more meaningful. "There's no sure formula to winning, but if there's one thing that every competitor who's ever won *The Challenge* can tell you, it's that you never quit, because the game is so unpredictable," she says. "It was so nice to get that first win off my back and to know that Veronica [Portillo] and I won together as best friends."

There was still so much more Rachel had left to learn, however. "Every season I did gave me such valuable lessons, whether it was about competition, or socially, or politically," she says. After *The Gauntlet*, "I remember coming into the next one thinking I was untouchable and that I could call out people if they weren't performing well." On *Battle of the Sexes 2*, she tried to publicly rally her team to vote off Katie Cooley (formerly Doyle) because, in her eyes, judging based on daily challenge performance was the fair way to decide who stays and who goes. Her plan backfired immediately, and Rachel was swiftly voted off instead. It was another eye-opening moment that reminded her how important politics are in the game, and that she needed to get better at making moves in secret rather than shouting her plans out loud.

She returned the next season for *The Inferno II* with a new appreciation and understanding of how to take control politically, and she worked with Veronica on the Bad Asses team to make sure she made it to the final. "Veronica and I are so dangerous together in a game, because we're smart and strong but don't play the game the way everyone wants us to," Rachel says. "We were ahead of our time, honestly. When you look back at *The Inferno II*, you see the boys trying to call the shots, and they all turned it into us being the 'mean girls.' That was really them trying to target us because we had all the power in the game, and none of the guys liked that."

Having all the political power can't guarantee a *Challenge* win, however. When the Bad Asses team lost to the Good Guys in the final that season, Rachel saw how attitude and team dynamics also impact the game. "Our team was like the Bad News Bears—none of us could get along," Rachel remembers. "People were having trouble running, and we were such a dysfunctional team, people were yelling, 'Fuck you! Run! Let's go!' while the other team was just so nice to each other. They really were the good guys, and it really came down to that. I think that show ended up the way it was meant to end up, so I wasn't that upset."

Rachel took a three-year hiatus from *The Challenge* after that season. When she returned for *The Island* in 2008, she once again saw how the game could bring out the worst in people as they'd do anything to win. But this time, the "good guys" were losing. "*The Island* was my first experience with extreme toxic masculinity," she says. "It was this weird experience where we didn't even have challenges. We just had to live on an island, and you could volunteer yourself into an elimination or just sit on the beach the whole time and starve, living in the constant berating and mocking from the guys going after Evelyn [Smith]. Then the villains won, and it was not okay. That's when I realized it's a fine line between winning and also recognizing that winning is not everything when it comes to just being a good person."

She didn't have enough political power to impact the game that season, but she still gave it her best shot anyway. She tried to make a big move by targeting Johnny "Bananas" Devenanzio, but it didn't work, and she was voted out in the third episode. "I love the moments where I fuck shit up on *The Island* because I went after who I wanted to," she says. "When I left, it was at least on my terms. I have no regrets because I didn't play with fear."

From that point forward, Rachel had a new mission on *The Challenge*. Winning was still as important to her as ever, but now she also vowed to make sure no one had a bad experience like *The Island* again if she could help it. "I know everyone had a good time on *The Duel II* when I was in a position of power," she says. "Nobody was feeling mocked, nobody was getting left out, nobody felt ostracized, for the most part. I was having so much fun. It was a feel-good season, and when you watch it, it's a feel-good show."

Rachel was also excited to see what she could accomplish in an individual season after being jealous of everyone who competed on the first *Duel* a few years prior. "When *The Duel II* came around, I knew that I didn't want to mess around anymore," she says. "I knew what to do. I was seasoned, I was experienced, I knew who was strong amongst the girls, and I knew who had to go in order for me to take the top." She considered Ruthie Alcaide to be her biggest competition that season, so she worked behind the scenes to take control of the "dodgeball"-style selection process. Rachel made sure Ruthie ended up in an early elimination, which she lost in a major upset. "I remember Ruthie leaving and literally saying to myself, 'You just won this show.'" She was right: after dominating the daily challenges all season, she went on to deliver one of the most impressive final performances of all time to earn her second *Challenge* championship. It wasn't even close. "That was my season," she says. "I didn't slow down when I was in first place, and I beat all the guys. That was my crowning moment."

By this point in her *Challenge* career, Rachel also understood that every season's theme, format, and cast list all have a massive impact on the game, and the way to succeed is by learning to adapt quickly. But she still wasn't prepared for how hard her experience would be when she returned for one more season three years later. "On *Battle of the Exes*, I had one of the lowest experiences that I ever had on a show," she says. She was partnered with her ex Aneesa Ferreira, and they were the only same-sex couple on the cast. "That was a really big undertaking for us, emotionally, socially, even on a representation level. I just remember feeling so unsupported. It would've made more sense if the teams were more evenly distributed, like there was a gay guy couple or maybe two lesbian teams—I don't know if they had the opportunity to do that, it was very experimental. I definitely think that it was a big lesson for me."

Rachel was struggling with going from the highs of feeling like she could trust a lot of people on *The Duel II* to all of a sudden feeling like no one wanted to see her and Aneesa succeed. "You know when you compete and no one cheers? That's how I felt," she remembers. "It's hard to break through that." She remembers withdrawing into herself and sleeping a lot that season to cope, and as a result, she isolated herself from her own partner when they should have been leaning on each other. It all came to a head during a daily challenge that was split into male and female rounds, and Rachel and Aneesa had the opportunity to use being the only same-sex couple to their advantage. "We were the only pair that could work together, and all I had to do was throw Aneesa a ball to let her pass the finish line first. I could have easily gotten another ball, but I missed that moment. That haunted me for a long time because it was my fault—I could have stepped up to give her more support and been a better partner. From that point on, I was very conscious of my role in the relationships. Was I supportive enough? How could I be better?"

Despite how difficult that season was for her to experience, she'd do it all over again in a heartbeat because she knew how important it was to show a lesbian couple on a show like *The Challenge*. As one of the earliest pioneers of LGBTQ+ representation in reality TV, she never took for granted the platform MTV gave her in that regard. "Twenty years ago I was coming out on *Road Rules*, kissing my girlfriend, and I didn't even think twice about it," she says. "To see the way younger kids look up to me, or seeing all the backlash for the LGBTQ community lately, I think to myself, we were so ahead of our time. Story lines have a major impact on cultural society, and I don't doubt that the fact that I was out on this show at a very early stage, wearing 'lesbian' across my chest on a T-shirt, meant something. But I really learned that there is a lot to still be done in terms of equality for gay people after *Exes*. I felt so alone in a house with nothing but heterosexual couples who have these certain dynamics. I just remember saying to myself, 'There's still a lot of work to be done and I have to do it.'"

That meant coming to terms with the fact that she also could have done even more in her time on *The Challenge*. While her close friendship with Veronica was well documented across multiple seasons, Aneesa revealed on *XXX: Dirty 30* that Rachel and Veronica had actually been in a serious relationship that was kept secret in front of the cameras for years. "Looking back now, having watched how the show has evolved, I do actually recognize that it was a missed opportunity in terms of representation," she says. "I mean, that could have had a huge impact." She explains that, at the time, she and Veronica decided their relationship was too special to be used as "house gossip" or portrayed as a showmance. "It was our business, and we knew if we did share it, it would become something that was not ours anymore. It would be this storyline on the show that everyone had two cents to put into. We wanted to protect it." But she's glad the truth finally came out. "People should know that we were in a relationship for years. We did live together. It was a big deal.

And we really had each other's backs and elevated each other into positions of winning. Even on the shows that she went on when I wasn't there, she was calling me, checking in, and there was a support system for the two of us for *The Challenge*."

After *Battle of the Exes*, Rachel was ready to move on from reality TV. "I had gotten what I wanted out of *The Challenge*, and I knew that I wanted to create a big life for myself outside of the show," she says. "I think a big part of being a winner in life is recognizing when it's time to start a new chapter and make new goals. I threw myself into my passion, which was fitness, and I created a career for myself starting from the ground up. I started training people out of my house, and I now have an online company that trains thousands of people a day and a subscription platform that is bigger than I could have ever even imagined. And now I'm doing workout specials for MTV, so it's like I'm throwing myself back into the *Challenge* world and it's all full circle."

She's also found herself thinking more and more about returning to *The Challenge* in an official capacity by competing in a season of *All Stars*. "I still have it in me, absolutely," she says. "I really do want to get my feet wet again, but I'm also a full-time mom. I have three kids under four." Taking that much time away just to add another win to her resume isn't as important to her as being the best wife and mom she can be for her family. "I have a very full life and I feel very blessed, and I really do look back at *The Challenge* and I thank it so much for how it helped me become that good life partner. It's all led me to where I am today. My advice to people is, don't let anyone else define what a champion is to you. I never did."

MARK LONG

Champion: *Real World/Road Rules Challenge,*
Battle of the Sexes

A lot of names have become synonymous with *The Challenge* over the years, but Mark Long is the true OG. Standing at six feet three inches and built with 230 pounds of intimidating muscle, he's one of the tallest and strongest players to ever compete on the show. The self-proclaimed *Challenge* Godfather has been around since its humble beginnings in the second season, which was the first time *The Challenge* featured a real competition between two teams, and he is the only person to have competed in all four decades the franchise has been on the air—the 1990s, 2000s, 2010s, and 2020s. "I've gone from being one of the first Challengers to literally one of the last, and hopefully that goes on for many more years," Mark says. "I mean, if I'm physically in shape, there's no reason why I shouldn't." He recently helped usher the franchise into a new era by campaigning on social media with the hashtag #WeWantOGs, kicking off the development of the *All Stars* spin-off, which brought so many fan-favorite competitors out of retirement. And with two championships to his name, he solidified his legacy in the

Challenge hall of fame a long time ago. But surprisingly, the Godfather's winning strategy actually has nothing to do with his physical abilities—he'd rather make an offer that no one can refuse, because to him, *The Challenge* is all about negotiating the best deal of his life.

Mark's reality TV career almost began in 1994, when he was in the running to be David "Puck" Rainey's replacement on *The Real World: San Francisco*. All these years later, he's still relieved that didn't work out, because his official reality TV debut on the first season of *Road Rules* a year later was much more his speed. "I was a three-sport high school athlete and was always more involved in competitive sports and active, rather than a *Real World* style of sitting in a house and doing nothing," Mark says. At the time, he was living in Los Angeles and working toward getting a broadcast journalism degree so he could become a TV host. "This was such a cool opportunity, and it could be how I get my foot in the door," he remembers thinking.

He had such a great experience as a founding member of *Road Rules* that when he got the call inviting him to help evolve *The Challenge* into an actual competition, he was on board immediately. The first season had featured five *Real World* alums traveling together and completing missions in a *Road Rules* format, but the second season was going to be very different. "I remember being told, 'We're going to do this challenge concept, and it's going to be *Real World* versus *Road Rules*, and there's going to be physical competitions and puzzles and craziness.' I thought that was the perfect, natural progression, and that was exactly what I wanted to do. I went in expecting to win."

The *Road Rules* team beat the *Real World* team in almost every single challenge that season, earning Mark his first *Chal-*

lenge championship. "We demolished them. I mean, it wasn't even close," he says. "I actually felt bad for them toward the end, knowing that my backpack was filled with money and theirs wasn't, but it's a competition." In his second season, 2002's *Battle of the Sexes*, Mark noticed how *The Challenge* had already evolved to even out the playing field and therefore raise the stakes of the competition. "Now they do the equalizers with the puzzles and the mind games, so it doesn't matter if you're male, female, big, little. They figured that out, and I think a lot of that started when we did *Battle of the Sexes*, because it was guys versus girls and they had to have some of those equalizers, because obviously, genetically, men are bigger than the girls."

With his impressive height, strength, and athletic abilities, Mark still could have easily relied on his physical attributes to do well. But if *The Challenge* was evolving, he realized he needed to evolve with it and create a strategy that no one else had. Instead of muscling his way through the competition, he decided to become an expert salesman and deal-maker, which is why he approached *Battle of the Sexes* as one massive sales pitch. "In the beginning, the *Challenge*s weren't strategic, and alliances didn't matter because it was a group of Road Rulers versus a group of Real Worlders," Mark says. "There wasn't a voting-off process back then. But as it evolved closer to what it is today, I found that *The Challenge* is the same thing as making a sale, and I see it as a six-week intensive sales pitch. Usually, there's two groups; you're either in this alliance or the other alliance. My job is to try to create a win-win plan for both sides where I don't look like a target, right? It's like, 'Hey, alliance A, I can promise you this, but in return, I want you to do that.' And then alliance B, my alliance, 'I will protect you from this as long as you don't do this to me.' I was a good facilitator of bridging the gap between alliances and always keeping the finger pointing away from myself."

It's a strategy that worked for the majority of Mark's *Challenge* career. He won *Battle of the Sexes* and would continue to make alliances and deals that successfully kept him out of eliminations for years (until he finally landed in his first one in *Battle of the Exes* in 2012). "I was crafty to use my sales skills and my strategy of controlling two different groups in a huge way to sell the idea that I should be kept around rather than person A, B, or C," he says. He always figured out ways to manipulate the game so he was in the exact position he wanted—even if that meant *not* making it to the final, like on *Battle of the Sexes 2* in 2004.

At the very beginning of that season, Mark created a secret alliance on his team called the Core Four with Eric Nies, Theo Vonkurnatowski, and Dan Setzler. That season's format required teams to nominate three captains for each challenge. If their team won, those three captains were safe and decided who out of the rest of their team would be sent home. If they lost the challenge, however, the rest of the team would decide which of the three captains would get eliminated. All season long, Mark's alliance made sure one of the four of them was always a captain. "Myself, Eric, Theo, and Dan pulled off this great strategy that no one ever noticed—there's not a challenge that went by where one of our Core Four is not in that group of three captains," he says. That way if the men lost the challenge, the three who weren't a captain would sway the rest of the team to vote one of the other two captains off instead. If the men won the challenge, the one who was a captain would convince the other two captains to vote out someone not in their alliance. "It's funny looking back on it, because we couldn't believe we fucking pulled it off. You couldn't have scripted it. The fans didn't even know about it because we were doing it internally. It worked seamlessly and made it one of my most fun *Challenge*s, because I always felt safe. I guarantee you it was the first time someone pulled off a season-long political strategy like that, for sure."

Mark was the only one from the Core Four alliance who didn't end up winning that season, but he says that was his own choice. He made a deal with the other three to fall on his sword and be the last guy voted out, allowing the rest of them to compete against the women in the final. In return, Mark got a portion of the prize money when Eric, Theo, and Dan eventually won. He doesn't regret giving up his spot in the final and therefore passing up the opportunity to get his third *Challenge* championship. In fact, the only regret he has from that season is when he had to send Brad Fiorenza home because he was the only guy left in the game who wasn't in the Core Four. "That really sucked, because I had really gotten to know and like Brad that season," Mark says. "It was, like, a day or two before the finals, and it was strictly because I had promised my allegiance to these guys before I even met Brad. When I sent Brad home, he hated me. He was pissed for years. It wasn't until I reached out to him and he eventually realized that it was just a strategy play and not a personal play, and we laugh about that today. He and I are best friends now."

Throughout all of Mark's *Challenge* career, that's the only time he ever felt guilty about a move he made in the game. "It did teach me that you can't promise everyone everything, because you never know how the game is going to go," he says. "I try to do my best to not promise too many people everything when I don't know the rules throughout the whole show, because that's a way to lose a friend right there if you're forced to break a promise. Over the past twenty-plus years, besides the Brad situation, I don't think I've ever left a *Challenge* where someone was like, 'Mark really screwed me.' I'm likable. I was never the villain. I'm genuine. I gave a shit about people. I didn't like sending people home, but it's part of the game."

When Mark returned for *The Gauntlet 2* in 2005, he pitched and sold himself flawlessly once again, safely maneuvering his way to the final on the Veterans team. But for the first time, he wasn't expecting to win. "People were so sick," Mark says. "I had the worst stomach flu ever, I was throwing up, and one of the stages was eating and I couldn't keep it down. Everyone was a wreck. I feel bad for production and [host] T.J. [Lavin] because our team gave up. We were so deflated just from how we felt."

After that disappointing end to the season, Mark decided to take a break from *The Challenge*. When he finally returned six seasons later for 2009's *The Duel II*, he was shocked to see just how much the franchise had evolved in his time away. He was still able to make deals and alliances that kept him out of eliminations, but he was not prepared for how much the final had changed. "I mean, you could knock out an older final in half a day, start to finish," he says. "As the money went up, the finals got harder. The *Duel II* final is when I realized it got serious. We covered so many miles biking and running. It was a bitch—I thought I tore an ACL three times during that challenge, it was that painful. I couldn't even go to the wrap party that night because my leg was elevated and I was icing it, thinking I was seriously injured. I was bedridden after that final for a good six hours. I couldn't walk."

Which is more iconic in *The Challenge* world: Mark or Mark's biceps?

For the majority of the season, Mark had been partnered up with his good friend and ally Rachel Robinson, but during the final he was forced to pair up with Aneesa Ferreira instead. Rachel ended up winning with Evan Starkman, and Mark and Aneesa finished in third place, in large part because Aneesa slowed him down. "Aneesa took a lot longer than everyone else, and I always get credit for not yelling like everyone else was doing to their female partners or berating them because they were slow; I'm just not built for that," Mark says. "I'm going to take it easy on Aneesa, and we're going to do this as friends and finish happy. And we did that. I get so many comments now like, 'You were so patient with Aneesa in the final,' and, 'You're such a gentleman,' and all this stuff, and I was proud of how I handled that moment. If my mom watched it, she'd be like, 'I raised a pretty good son.' I didn't look back on it like, 'Aneesa really screwed me!' I look back on it as, 'Good for her for not giving up and allowing me to be able to finish. If she gave up, they would have driven me to the finish line in a van.' But it would have been cool if Rachel showed up first and she and I went and kicked ass for the rest of the final."

Mark had yet another close call five seasons later on *Battle of the Exes* (in what would become his last-ever appearance on the main franchise). After working all season in a tight alliance with Johnny "Bananas" Devenanzio and Camila Nakagawa, Mark and his partner/ex, Robin Hibbard, were forced to go head-to-head with them in the last elimination before the final. Johnny and Camila won the physical matchup, but Mark says "there were a lot of things people don't see" that led to that outcome. He didn't think his partner would have been able to handle the final. "Robin was mentally checked out," he says. "She just had enough. I don't think I even would have done well on that final, to be honest with you, because we were attached with our partner. I'm glad Johnny won—I mean, I should definitely get half of that win. If we're being honest, he should have six and a half wins and I should have two and a half wins. Read between the lines there. I made every final that I've wanted to make, let's put it that way."

Despite not returning to the main franchise after *Battle of the Exes*, Mark's biggest *Challenge* win was yet to come. He started his own production company, selling TV shows using the skills he'd learned and honed over his years as a competitor. And then the ultimate *Challenge* salesman helped bring the ultimate *Challenge* pitch to life by campaigning for *All Stars*. "What's crazy is I just threw out a simple tweet saying, 'Who'd be up for an all-OG *Challenge*, shorter season, shorter shooting schedule, nice and easy?' That's it," Mark says. "And before I knew it, the tweet went viral." Once news stories were written about his social media campaign, it was further proof that this idea was a surefire hit, so he reached out to Bunim/Murray Productions before shopping it around to other companies. "I said, 'Look, if you guys don't do this, don't be mad at me when I take it somewhere else and this thing is a huge hit. Out of respect for my BMP family, I want to make a deal with you guys, but I've had other high-level people reach out to me that have done competition shows that want to do this show.' I wanted to get it going because I knew there was an audience for it."

Within eight months, the dream became a reality, and the first season of *The Challenge: All Stars* premiered on the new streaming service Paramount+ in 2021. Mark's idea of leaning into nostalgia and fun set *All Stars* apart from the increasingly intense main franchise, and the first season was a smash hit with fans, competitors, and even T.J., who served as host. Since then, *All Stars* has successfully delivered three seasons (and counting). "There's not one person that says anything negative about *All Stars*," Mark says. "It's always like, 'This is the fucking greatest. Please don't ever stop.' Critics who don't hold back on anything love it, saying things like *All Stars* is giving all the other reality shows a master class in how TV should be."

At the beginning of *All Stars*, Mark was involved solely as a producer. He personally reached out to about eighty different potential cast members and intended to work on that first season behind the scenes. Eventually MTV asked him to join the cast, however, so he stepped back from his day-to-day producer duties to keep things fair. "After that, I didn't know the format, I didn't know the challenges we were going to be doing, I didn't know the final cast," he says. When he arrived in Argentina, he was eager to prove that even though he was involved in developing the spin-off, he wasn't getting a free ride to the final.

He got his chance near the end of the season when he was sent into an exhausting elimination partnered with Kendal Darnell (formerly Sheppard), and they won against Laterrian Wallace and Katie Cooley (formerly Doyle). "That was one of the coolest moments for me, because I felt like since I rallied that show into existence, this was my moment to prove to everyone that I deserve to be there and I'm going to fight for it."

Immediately after that elimination victory, Mark ended up winning the last daily challenge of the season, which guaranteed his spot in the final. "I'm the oldest one there, and I was rubbing it in all those younger guys' faces," Mark says. "That was so cool. I loved how I proved that I earned my spot there." The final was more difficult than any of the cast members were expecting, especially ones who hadn't competed in many years, but Mark is proud that everyone crossed the finish line. "I was a mess after that final. I mean, talk about being sleep deprived and hungry and dirty—and I was wearing Invisalign at the time, throughout the whole final. I was getting sand in my mouth. It was gross. But even if it took me longer to finish, I always knew that I wasn't giving up. I am not built for quitting." Mark finished *All Stars* in fifth place, and when he returned for *All Stars 3*, he didn't add another championship to his resume but is still proud of how he competed. "I had a rough go on *All Stars 3*, but I am undefeated in eliminations on *All Stars*. They can never take that from me, baby," he says with a laugh.

The future holds a lot of promise—and not just for Mark. He hopes to see *The Challenge* continue to grow, evolve, and expand on both the main franchise and *All Stars*, and he's got a dream for how the two can eventually come together. "[As of this book's writing] we're getting ready for season thirty-eight of *The Challenge*," Mark says. "Season forty is a big number, so it would be the perfect time to do something like the younger cast versus the OGs, like a Super Bowl of *Challenge*s. It would be the biggest *Challenge* they've done yet, and I've talked to a lot of the older folks and they're down. I'm training for that. It will be so epic. That's the evolution of where *The Challenge* should go." Sold!

TYLER DUCKWORTH

Champion: *Cutthroat, Rivals*

When Tyler Duckworth began his reality TV experience on *The Real World: Key West* in 2005, the franchise already meant a lot to him because of what it showed him when he watched it as a kid. "I knew I was gay from a very young age. Being where I was from, it was seeing these people telling their life stories on *The Real World* that gave me the perspective that there's a bigger, wider world out there," he says. "When I got older, I wanted to maybe be that for someone else." He's proud of the way he got to showcase his true personality as a young gay man on his *Real World* season, but the experience of filming was more difficult and emotionally exhausting than he expected. That's why he didn't intend to return to reality television once he got home.

When he got the call to go on *The Duel* in 2006, however, he found strength in numbers. His *Key West* castmates Johnny "Bananas" Devenanzio, Paula Beckert (formerly Meronek), and Svetlana Shusterman had also been invited, and they all agreed to go into the season as an alliance and hopefully break the infamous streak of rookies being eliminated first. But the season's new format threw them for a loop, and they quickly realized that their alliance couldn't save them from being targeted—and Tyler was selected to go into the first elimination. "It was just a rude awakening for my first *Challenge*," he says. "I remember Johnny and I both looking at each other that first day being like, 'What did we get ourselves into?'"

Tyler did the exact thing he was trying to avoid when he called out his own ally Johnny as his elimination opponent. "I knew that they were going after Key West regardless, so I called in my own roommate, but you should never target your own alliance," he says. "I had to make a snap judgment. In hindsight, I did it because I knew him well enough to know I could beat him, truth be told. I should have taken a moment, taken a step back to just breathe and think, but I panicked." After beating Johnny and sending him home, Tyler had a chance to make a better move when he was immediately selected again to go into the second elimination. This time, he went for one of the bigger threats with whom he was not aligned—Derrick Kosinski—but was defeated. "I'm glad that I went for a big dog even though I lost," he says.

His time on *The Duel* ended quicker than he anticipated, but it came with some hard-earned lessons. Tyler now knew the importance of thinking through every decision, sticking with his alliance, and making big moves, regardless of how terrifying they may be. He couldn't play to not fail; he had to play to win. And watching his *Key West* castmate Janelle Casanave win the next season, *The Inferno 3*, proved to him that he could do it, too, so he tried again on *The Gauntlet III* in 2008. "I was just so happy to get the call. But despite the fact that I was always an athlete, I wasn't in great shape and I didn't come in feeling physically or mentally like I was there," he says. "And I also wasn't prepared for the fact that Johnny was going to do whatever it took for him to get me off the show—and he had every right to be salty about what had happened on *The Duel*."

While Tyler previously had his epiphany about not turning on your allies, Johnny was still on the hunt for his own revenge. "In hindsight, all of us can laugh now, but Paula, Janelle, me, and Johnny should have been running that game together," Tyler says. "But Johnny was just so consumed with getting back at me that he spoiled his own game and then he screwed Paula." The conditions on *Gauntlet III* also contributed to Tyler having a terrible time that season. "It wasn't fun like the first one. I didn't feel like I had any friends. The other gay guy there, Ryan [Kehoe], totally played me, and I allowed myself to get played. I didn't really want to be there."

After *The Gauntlet III*, Tyler was once again ready to put his reality TV days behind him. He was still hurting from what he considered to be a "tough edit" from his *Real World* season, and he was out early on his first two seasons of *The Challenge*. But when he got the call to come back for *Cutthroat* in 2010, he was in better physical shape because he'd been lifting weights and teaching spin classes, and he felt supported by people at his work who were cheering him on. He'd also watched *The Challenge* during his break from the show and had a better grasp of how to play the social and political game. He saw how other castmates had bad blood from previous seasons while he had a clean slate by comparison, which could help him potentially slide under the radar. "I came ready to play in a way that I hadn't before. I took it seriously as a competition for the first time. I had no other agenda other than I was there to win and I was ready to show it."

He just had no idea he'd have to prove himself as intensely as he did toward the end of the season when, in one of the biggest twists in *Challenge* history, producers brought in C.T. Tamburello as a mercenary to go against Tyler and Johnny in an elimination. "I was ready to go against Bananas, and we were like, 'Let's just squash this beef now and then it'll be done,'" he says. "But for them to just march C.T. out randomly, Johnny and I were looking at each other like, 'What the fuck? How is this happening right now?'"

Thanks to a lucky coin flip, Johnny had to go against C.T. first in Back Up Off Me, leading to one of the most iconic eliminations ever. Strapped back-to-back with Johnny, C.T. stood up and sumo-stomped his way to the finish line, using Johnny's body to knock over the barrel in a moment that appropriately became known as the Bananas Backpack. "Looking back, I'm so happy to have been a part of it because that's *Challenge* history, but to see a brother of yours—even though he was a nemesis at the time—just get destroyed in seconds, you're like, 'Oh, shit. It's my turn,'" Tyler says. "It's terrifying being harnessed to C.T. We had no time to prepare for this, and now I had to face the biggest, baddest competitor in *Challenge* history."

Tyler knew he had a slight advantage, since he only had to outlast Johnny's time of nineteen seconds—which he did. But it turns out that Tyler didn't just take the win after twenty seconds. "The funny thing is, and you can ask anyone that was there that day, I went against C.T. for forty-five minutes," he says. "I was absolutely showboating—I just wanted to let every other guy in that cast know what I could do." It was only after Tyler's teammate Brad Fiorenza yelled from the sidelines that he needed to conserve his energy for the last daily challenge of the season that Tyler finally stopped fighting. "I had already won, but it was more of a pride thing after such a low low on *Gauntlet III*. And my confidence went from two to a thousand percent."

Tyler found himself back in an elimination immediately, the last one of the season, against Derrick, who had previously beaten him on *The Duel*—but he wasn't worried. "When you are harnessed against C.T. and then you do that, it's like, I can do anything now. I had won that *Challenge* during that elimination," he says. He beat Derrick and went into the final knowing he was going to come out of it as a champion. "I just kept on remembering: 'You've done the work, so if not you, then who? If not now, when? You've earned that final. You're not going to lose it.'" He knew he could handle whatever was thrown at him, and as long as his teammates could keep up, he didn't see the other two teams as any real competition. "I was calling the shots at that point for our team, and I was pacing us as if the other teams were right behind us. I was like, 'We've got to pretend like they're behind us the whole time.' But we won it by six hours."

After two tough seasons of *The Challenge*, Tyler had used everything he had learned to finally win, and the moment he held the giant check on top of the castle in Prague made his previous struggles worth it. "All my friends were shocked when they saw me win, just because it's always the gay guy that gets thrown into eliminations first, and gay guys don't win *Challenge*s," he says. "And they don't win them in the fashion that I had won it, against those types of competitors. I felt like I was showing the gay community in a positive way, that gay guys are not only worthy competitors but also that they can win. And I was hungry to show that even more. But after *Cutthroat*, I felt a lot more pressure on my shoulders to perform."

During the *Cutthroat* final, he saw how important it was both to support his teammates and to lean on them, no matter who they were. It was the perfect preparation for when he returned the next season for *Rivals* in 2011. Based on everyone's preseason conversations, Tyler and Johnny predicted the format (that people would be paired up with their worst enemy) and that they'd be each other's partner. So before they even arrived in Costa Rica, they decided to bury the hatchet and start off as a strong, unified team. "Johnny had been like, 'If we are going to be teammates, we have to just figure it out,'" Tyler says. "He apologized and said how proud he was of me for winning *Cutthroat*, and I thanked him for his advice telling me to take charge of my team."

Had C.T. not come in as a mercenary during *Cutthroat*, and had the Bananas Backpack not happened, Tyler isn't sure that their honest pre-*Rivals* conversation could have happened. "I don't know how well Johnny and I would've gotten along, and because of the Bananas Backpack, he had more beef against C.T. than me, so that created an opportunity for us to heal and have a common enemy in C.T.," he says. "But when I got there—my god. I was more scared than ever. If you look at that cast, they were all [giants]. I started getting in my head. I thought everyone would think my *Cutthroat* win was a fluke." It was thanks to Johnny's constant support and coaching that Tyler was able to calm down enough to perform well. "We picked beds next to each other. We shared protein shakes every day. Johnny was like my RuPaul. He was like, 'No inner saboteur. Get out of your head. You're an amazing competitor. You earned that victory, and we can win this if we just stay focused.'"

That's not to say that Tyler and Johnny were perfect partners. Tyler still found himself facing a lot of the same issues that caused him and Johnny to become enemies in the first place. "He's really obnoxious. He is a caricature of himself times ten," Tyler says. "But I knew I had to take a step back and look at the bigger picture, because if he wins, I win, and if I win, he wins. And we won *a lot* of challenges."

Despite how well they were doing, Tyler and Johnny knew not to count their prize money before they earned it. They'd both suffered hard losses in previous seasons and knew how quickly their game could end. "Every single week, it was just: survive," he says. "Make it to the next challenge. When it came to the voting, if you're up on the chopping block, don't say anything." But their worst nightmare still came true when they were betrayed by their own friend and ally Paula and were thrown into the final elimination of the season against C.T. and his partner, Adam King. "I was so angry, and Johnny threw his helmet. We never thought Paula would be the deciding vote to put us into the final elimination."

Instead of dwelling on their fears, Tyler remembered how winning the last elimination before the final on *Cutthroat* had turned out to be the best thing for him, so he took charge of their team in the eleventh hour. "When we were on the bus, Johnny was feeling defeated, and I was like, 'No matter what happens, we can be so proud of what we've done already,'" Tyler says. "And he was like, 'Yeah, but it's C.T. and we both know what happened last time.' I was like, 'So let's write new history.'"

Staying in that mindset proved difficult when they walked into the elimination set and saw two deep trenches dug into the dirt that intersected in the middle and realized this was going to be full-contact. "I saw football gear and I was like, 'Oh god. Oh no.' C.T. was jacked at the time, and then you see him in football gear and he was all hyped. Johnny was terrified and thought it was over before it started." And it almost was, since, during the elimination, Tyler grabbed the wrong ball in the beginning and had to double back to correct his mistake, losing precious seconds. "But Adam made the exact same mistake simultaneously, and mind you, Adam and I are arguably the two most intelligent people to ever have been on a *Challenge*, but we were both being directed by our partners. Johnny corrected my error instead of getting mad at me, and Adam made so many more errors at that point, and it all came down to our communication."

In order to give his teammate more time to catch up, C.T. decided to run full speed into Johnny and Tyler in the middle of the trench—*"Choo choo!"*—and he did some real damage. "I remember it hurting so much," Tyler says. "But you just keep on running. I was borderline concussed at that point, and I had no idea it was that close." In the final seconds, Tyler and Adam were racing to each score their final point, and both guys were completely gassed to the point where they were crawling in the dirt up the trench. "I had nothing left, just wiggling up the hill. It was almost like a Hollywood screwball comedy from the twenties. But I got up first, and you hear this eruption, and I knew we had won."

It's one of the moments that Tyler is most proud of from his *Challenge* career, because he knows he and Johnny should have lost that elimination. "If you look at size and speed, it was them all the way, and this did not play to any of our strengths other than communication," Tyler says. "Instead of C.T. being so distracted about getting in my way or Johnny's way, he should have been helping Adam correct his errors, where Johnny immediately was able to talk me through mine. That's why we were able to win. And it showed that Johnny had complete faith in me to do it in the end because he didn't try to pull me up by *my* shorts. I did it on my own. It was just so poetic after *Cutthroat* with Johnny and me and C.T."

Once again, Tyler was victorious against C.T. right before a final, and now Johnny knew what that felt like, too. And just like with *Cutthroat*, Tyler knew there was no way he was losing the *Rivals* final. "It gives you that extra confidence going into the final. It tested me; it woke me back up again. I already won when me and Johnny settled the score with C.T. and became friends again. I was going in with a really solid attitude."

It didn't hurt that Tyler didn't see the other two male teams left as threats. "The team I was more scared of other than C.T. was actually Wes [Bergmann] and Kenny [Santucci], but they had been doing so poorly all season," Tyler says. "And then you had Leroy [Garrett] and his partner, Mike [Ross], which was *Challenge* 101: bring a bad team to the final. I was just looking at the competitors at that point, and Johnny and I both said to each other, 'We're playing with house money.' I was walking around with swagger."

But then disaster struck the night before the final began. "We went to this shady restaurant in Argentina, and I swear to god, it was where hikers and skiers go to do shrooms," Tyler says. "I'll eat anything, so Jenn [Grijalva] and I go ham on the charcuterie plate while everyone else just drank. And who gets sick? Me and Jenn. I was up all night. I couldn't get any fluids in me. A cameraman found me in the kitchen the next morning lying naked on the cold floor holding a garbage bag. It was coming out both ends. It was so gross. This is not how I thought the final was going to start."

As the other players were getting their uniforms on the next morning, Tyler and Jenn were getting checked out by the doctor. Johnny tried to cheer up Tyler by pointing out how hot the male doctor was, but Tyler was feeling so sick that he didn't even care. And when the doctor recommended that Tyler wasn't medically fit to continue, he refused to quit even though he had never felt so sick. "We had sacrificed everything just to get to that point, so absolutely, I was going to try," he says. "But I hadn't slept, and I had thrown up everything in my system, so production gave me, like, three and a half hours to eat saltine crackers and drink Gatorade and try to get back up to speed. We started in a lake, and anything water related, I knew I was going to be fine. We just had to not be in last."

In the beginning, Tyler let Johnny take control because he was so dehydrated that he could barely think straight. He gives Johnny a lot of credit for going easy on him at such a crucial moment. "Johnny does have this very caring side to him, and he was just so kind and tempered," he says. "I was just like, 'Tell me what to do and I'll do it.' And we ended up catching up to Wes and Kenny in the canoe portion." Back then, there had never been a two-day final on *The Challenge*, so Tyler and Johnny thought the race would end on that first day, which only helped motivate them even more. "Johnny saw that I had so much heart and so much fight in me, and we thought the finish line was close." Not even getting the memory portion— where they had to re-create an entire campsite perfectly after a long run—wrong multiple times (more than what was shown on TV) deterred Tyler, even though he remembers each failed check as "soul crushing." And somehow, after all that, when they began the long hike up the mountain, Tyler found his strength coming back just as Johnny began to lose his.

"I was like, 'Johnny, just pace yourself and make sure that Wes and Kenny are within eyesight so if we get to the finish line, we can sprint,'" Tyler says. "And when we got to the eating part, I was so hungry and Johnny got this glimmer in his eye. We saw Wes crying. We saw Paula crying. Kenny was crying. Everyone was crying and throwing up and I was just like, 'Food!' because we could not eat that whole day. And everyone on the crew was waiting to see Tyler Duckworth do an eating challenge."

For Tyler, eating pound after pound of the Argentinian feast wasn't the punishment it was for all the other competitors. He treated it as replenishing the energy he so badly needed, and now he was ready to finish out the final that night—or so he thought. "I think we caught up three hours on Wes and Kenny," he says. "And then we were just stalking them slowly. At one point, I saw Wes being carried by Kenny, and that gave me even more incentive and strength to know that he was dying. But there was a puzzle that they didn't show [on TV] that we messed up on, so we thought we had gotten second place, and we were fine with that."

After the puzzle, Tyler and Johnny actually stopped, dropped the weight they were carrying, and sat down to watch the sun set and bask in what they thought was their second-place finish, not realizing they were only approaching the end of day one. "It's one of the most touching, beautiful moments of my life," Tyler says. They finished the hike only to see Paula crying on a rock with no check in hand, and Tyler realized it wasn't over. "At that moment, I was like, 'We can do this, there's still a chance.' And that second day was what I was built to do."

The next morning, as they finished the climb up the mountain only minutes behind Wes and Kenny, Tyler found himself coaching Johnny, the opposite of how they operated on the first day. "I would time out two minutes that we'd climb, and then I gave him a fifteen-second break and then we'd keep on going. We caught up so much ground that we were ahead of Wes and Kenny when we got to the top," Tyler says. "They were so frustrated and angry. And the gag of the season was T.J. is like, 'Use this GPS and find a key and then run to the top of the mountain.' I was not as fast as Wes or Kenny or Johnny, so Johnny's like, 'Tyler, just run!' Wes and Kenny are literally fighting over who gets to use the GPS, and I'm already making a beeline up the mountain as if I found the key. Johnny finds the key and we race up and beat all the other teams."

Suffering from food poisoning, feeling more dehydrated and exhausted than he'd ever been in his life, and finishing the first day behind the other team didn't matter to Tyler when he and Johnny crossed the finish line and won *Rivals*. "I started crying," Tyler says. "I was thinking about all those competitors that I was terrified of when I showed up at the beginning who were the best of all time, and we had picked them off one by one and we had earned this victory. No one can ever take this away from us. And the night before, when we thought we had lost, we had that cathartic moment where we let our emotions out with each other, and that made the win even more special."

Winning *Rivals* proved to Tyler how good things happen when you put in the work, no matter how impossible it may seem. And setting their differences aside and communicating with each other were the keys to Tyler and Johnny's success. "No matter what was thrown at us, we were able to find that victory," Tyler says. "And on a personal note, all those inner saboteurs in my head were gone because I went against two of the biggest dogs in *Challenge* history and won. It's still a fever dream to me, literally."

When he got home, Tyler realized he couldn't lose if he kept that mindset going in his real life. "I was a lot more confident in terms of making asks at work, going after those promotions and raises and taking those bigger steps," he says. "That was always hard for me—I don't know if it's just because of who I am or being a gay guy from my generation, but I was always questioning my worth. 'Am I good enough?' But going through those hardships physically and mentally and emotionally and spiritually, I knew I could handle anything. It gave me a new backbone." He also learned to never doubt his choices or regret any mistakes he might make, because everything that happened on his first two seasons of *The Challenge* led to him winning his second two. "I needed to go through what I went through to get to where I needed to. I don't think I would've won those two *Challenge*s had I not gone through those lows." And now, as a middle and high school teacher, he also finds ways to pass all those lessons on to his students. "I've turned it academic. I make allegorical comparisons about World War Two or invasions to *The Challenge* stuff. It's fun because my students will dig up videos and be like, 'Mr. Duckworth, you used to have abs!' And I'm like, 'Hey, I still do. I'm getting back in shape!'"

While Tyler hasn't been able to win again since he's returned for multiple seasons of the *All Stars* spin-off, he's having more fun than ever, and to him, that's worth even more than another *Challenge* championship. "If you go on *The Challenge* looking for something other than the victory, you're going to find so much more in that process," he says. "I've made amazing friends and I was able to be vulnerable and fully be me for the first time on TV—I would never ever have done drag on *Cutthroat* or *Rivals*. I'm doing things that terrify me and it keeps on getting better, so maybe that's the secret—for both the *Challenge* and life. It's a lot simpler than you think."

CARA MARIA SORBELLO

**Champion: *Battle of the Bloodlines*, *Vendettas*
(plus *Champs vs. Pros*)**

On paper, Cara Maria Sorbello is the definition of a *Challenge* GOAT. Out of the fourteen seasons she's been on, she made it to *nine* finals—the most of any female competitor ever. She's won twice on the main franchise and once on the *Champs vs. Pros* spin-off. And her elimination record is downright intimidating, with thirteen wins and only six losses, the most elimination wins by a woman ever. But unlike every other elite *Challenge* winner with similar resumes, Cara Maria doesn't come from a sports background. She never had any athletic skills or experience at all. She wasn't even social growing up. Logically, her *Challenge* career should have ended after her disastrous rookie season, when she was eliminated first from 2010's *Fresh Meat II* with her partner, Darrell Taylor. But instead, she's become one of the best players of all time.

It's a journey that's taken even Cara Maria herself by surprise. When she was in college, she submitted an application for *The Real World* on a whim. But since casting for *The Real World* had closed, she was offered a callback for *Bad Girls Club* instead. "I'm a straight-A student, I don't do drugs, I don't party, I'm not getting hammered and getting into fights. I'm a good girl!" she says. "I was like, why would they even want me on a show like this?" She still went to the casting meeting in the hopes that they'd like her enough to consider her for a different show, because she clearly did not meet the requirements for a *Bad Girls Club* cast member. "I'm looking around and I'm like, I don't belong here," she says. "They asked me, 'Have you ever fought with a girl?' 'No, I just go and brush my horse on the weekend.'" And yet, she somehow still kept getting callbacks for *Bad Girls Club*. It got far enough into the casting process that she eventually had to tell them she wasn't interested in joining that particular show. Speaking up worked out in her favor: while she didn't end up on *The Real World* like she had originally intended, she was ultimately invited to join *The Challenge* for *Fresh Meat II*. She had no idea what the show was about, but as long as it wasn't *Bad Girls Club*, she was on board.

By this time, Cara Maria had finished college and was working as a bartender in Hollywood, so she told her coworkers she'd be gone for two months to film . . . which only confused them when she returned just a week later. "They were like, 'Did you even leave?' I was like, 'I don't want to talk about it,'" she says. "I thought [the producers] were never going to invite me back again. But I think the best stories come from the hardest beginnings, and that's my story."

Her swift failure on *Fresh Meat II* was eye-opening for her in a lot of ways. She didn't have any experience being around large groups, and suddenly she was living in a house with twenty-five rowdy, hard-partying people with big personalities who were, by definition, her enemies, all trying to get her out of the game. "It was just getting thrown into the snake pit right away," she says. "I didn't have anyone who had my back, and then on top of that, I was learning the social aspect, learning what it's like to even be on TV, and figuring out what *The Challenge* was without knowing anything about sports . . . it was a lot. I had to learn a lot and grow a lot from that."

That's why Cara Maria cringes if she ever sees footage from her first season, especially her blowup the night before her elimination when everyone else was partying and she was trying to sleep. "I took everything so personally. I was annoyed that people were up partying when I had an elimination the next day, because I had no concept of how this all worked," she says. "I didn't realize that because I had done the best in the combines, with the exception of the puzzle, that meant I was the threat for the girls. And then Darrell was the multi-time champion, so of course they wanted to get rid of us."

As soon as she got home, she did her research. "I started watching old seasons of *The Challenge*, and that's when I realized the shit they do," she says. "It was terrifying, but I was like, 'I have to do this. I have to get better.'" She was given a second chance the following season on *Cutthroat* and felt more prepared this time around, though the other competitors still had low expectations of her. She was thrown into an early elimination against Mandi Moyer, and everyone immediately wrote Cara Maria off. "Mandi was part of the cool group, and I remember me and Mandi got into it in the kitchen, and they were all talking about how Mandi's just going to steamroll me and it's going to be game over. I realized that no one had any faith in me whatsoever. And that just pissed me off."

A fire that she'd never felt before was lit inside her all of a sudden. "Just out of sheer anger, I went into the backyard, which was huge, and I started running laps while everybody was in the hot tub," she remembers. "I was like, I'm just going to keep going. I want them to be checking their watches, drinking their wine, like, 'How is she still running?' And I kept running and running and running and running until finally somebody stopped me." She stayed angry all the way through the elimination the next night, and for the first time, she found the fierce competitor that she never knew was inside of her when she demolished Mandi in a purely physical battle. "What I didn't have in athletics and what I didn't have in knowing how to be around people, I had in heart, and that was the trigger for me in unlocking it," she says. "I gave everything I had, and I was so proud of myself. I remember thinking, 'I've never done anything like that ever before. And I want to keep doing it.'"

And so Cara Maria, the ultimate underdog, was officially born. Season after season, she found herself with little or no allies and thrown in eliminations, and her abilities were consistently underestimated. But she figured out how to stop taking it personally and use it as fuel for success instead. "I found out that I thrive as an underdog," she says. "That feeling that nobody believes in you and nobody thinks you could do it, it makes me go, 'Watch me. I'll prove you wrong.'" That season was a major turning point for her, because not only did she find her stride as an elimination beast, but she also proved herself as a major *Challenge* threat in finals by finishing in second place on *Cutthroat* (even as her own team doubted her ability to cross the finish line), as well as on the next season, *Rivals* (with her partner, Laurel Stucky), and then on *Rivals II* (with partner Heather Cooke).

Coming so close to victory multiple times may have been discouraging, but Cara Maria didn't let it completely dishearten her. Just like she used her haters as fuel, she used her losses as inspiration to come back again and again and push herself even harder. "Every time I would fail at something, I'd be like, 'I'm going to be better. I'm going to do better,'" she says. "And for a girl like me, who has, like, one friend, I don't have an athletic bone in my body, I just have a lot of heart, as cheesy as it is, I wanted to prove to everyone that anyone could do it. As the girl that nobody ever believed in, who didn't even believe in myself, I wanted to show that anything is possible."

And after Emily Schromm "humbled the shit out of" her in the X Battle elimination on *Battle of the Exes*, Cara Maria was inspired to find a new kind of strength—literally. She started doing CrossFit training and discovered how powerful she could really be if she put in the work, and she showcased that new power on *Free Agents* in 2014. Along with the house politics not being on her side (as usual), luck was also not working in her favor that season, since she kept flipping the Kill Card in the Draw and had to compete in four eliminations. Her first one was a hard-fought endurance battle that lasted an hour and a half, which she won inch by inch as she pulled Nia Moore across the dirt to her bell. Cara Maria showed everyone on the sidelines (and those watching from home) that she had reached new heights physically to match her never-give-up attitude. And she continued to let her haters fuel her fire: as Johnny "Bananas" Devenanzio cheered loudly against Cara Maria, she used that as inspiration to get her second (and third, fourth, and fifth) wind before finally ringing the bell and sending Nia home.

Somewhere along the way, thanks to her attitude and improved performance, her allies started to outnumber her enemies. It might have been from watching her emerge victorious from elimination after elimination on *Free Agents*. Or maybe it was seeing her refuse to quit even after breaking her hand and continuing to compete with a cast on near the end of that season. But Cara Maria's competitors finally started to root for her, too. It was one of the most rewarding moments of her *Challenge* career, because she'd fought so hard for so long on her own, and now it was finally paying off. She gained allies like C.T. Tamburello, who was willing to partner with her on a daily challenge right before the final, even though one of her hands was wrapped in a cast—potentially risking his own safety in the game—because he knew she would never quit on him. She had people sticking up for her when Laurel, her friend at the time, wasn't treating her with respect, showing how far she'd come with her social politics. She eventually lost to Laurel in an elimination because her cast hindered her performance, but she says she doesn't regret her season ending because of an injury. "I wouldn't take back that my hand was broken, because the way everything played out inspired a lot of people and showed me what I was capable of. The only thing I wish I could change was figuring out a way to do better in that elimination, even with the cast."

After seven seasons full of life-changing experiences and close calls, Cara Maria was more than ready to win. And she finally did secure her first *Challenge* championship on *Battle of the Bloodlines* in 2015, partnered with her cousin Jamie Banks. It should have been one of the happiest moments of her life, but it came with a lot of baggage instead. Her grandmother, whom she was very close to, had passed away right before filming began. And then during the season, Cara Maria decided to end her relationship with her then long-term boyfriend, Abram Boise, whom she had met on *Cutthroat*. She described the relationship as "unhealthy" while talking about it to her cousin and admitted to kissing castmate Thomas Buell before Abram joined the cast midseason as a replacement. Everything blew up at the *Bloodlines* reunion show, and she feels it overshadowed her long-awaited win. "*Bloodlines* was very hard on me mentally, and there's a lot of things that I had to overcome that season, and unfortunately, that was the main thing, not my win," she says. "It was a lot to go through mentally, and just so traumatic."

But she approached everything that she was going through,

both on and off the show, the same way that she did in that pivotal elimination against Nia: "Just keep inching forward. You'll get there eventually, one step at a time. The pain will end if you just keep pushing." With how much she'd grown, now things that previously seemed impossible—like jumping out of a plane during the final on *XXX: Dirty 30* despite being deathly afraid of heights—she found she could actually handle. Sure, she didn't *want* to jump (and she cried the whole way down, too), but she didn't quit. "It always comes down to the fact that if you don't think you can do it, you won't. There's no secret. You just have to do the work."

That's how Cara Maria was finally able to redeem her original *Fresh Meat II* performance by winning *Champs vs. Pros* with Darrell in 2017, earning $55,000 for the ASPCA, her charity of choice, and beating Olympians and professional athletes along the way. "Nothing could take away from that win," she says. "That was just so meaningful and epic." That experience gave her the final boost of confidence she needed to go on to become the individual winner of *Vendettas* in 2018, making her the only female solo winner of

Cara's used to fighting on her own, so it's fitting she's the only solo female winner of *The Challenge*.

The Challenge. She didn't have to face a single elimination that season, because she had finally earned respect from the male competitors, who wanted to work with her rather than send her home. "I'd finally established myself as a competitor in their eyes, which felt amazing. But little did they know they'd have to run against me at the end," she says. "And I remember I have never felt so good running a final. I blew them all away. But unfortunately, I got attacked for most of the reunion. Both *Bloodlines* and *Vendettas* meant so much to me because of how much I fought in each of them, how much I went through mentally, and then both wins were unfortunately overshadowed. Both wins came with a little hurt."

She didn't understand how she had somehow gone from the underdog everyone rooted for to the frontrunner no one wanted to see win. But the difference was, now she refused to let it get to her like she used to. "Fuck it, however it happened, I won. The check cashed," she says. "And I had so much fun competing on *Vendettas*, so I'm so mad now looking back that I let any of those guys make me cry. I'm looking back on the experiences I've been through, both on and off the show. I let a lot of actions and behaviors roll off my back, and a lot of it's starting to come to light. And I know that even though bad things happened, I'm not a victim. I am strong. My experiences are valid, and I can overcome anything."

Cara Maria wants to show her fans—and her haters, too, always—that no matter what she's been through, she's stronger for it. And in turn, she hopes to keep inspiring others who may be struggling in similar ways, either dealing with toxic relationships or being bullied or made to feel like they don't deserve what they've earned. "I just really want to help other people at the end of the day, through my own experiences, and for people to realize when things are not okay, you shouldn't accept it."

And she knows she's still learning herself, especially after her last *Challenge* appearance on *War of the Worlds 2* in 2019. After dominating the season by maintaining the majority alliance and controlling the house politics, Cara Maria and the rest of Team USA lost in a major upset in the last leg of the final. She also alienated a lot of her fellow cast members as a result, and she saw how the public's opinion of her shifted. While it's one of the most heartbreaking losses she's ever experienced, she understands why other players and fans dubbed her the "villain" of the season and nicknamed her alliance "Cara's Cult"—though she's quick to give all credit to Paulie Calafiore and Kam Williams for orchestrating their giant alliance. She realized that when she's no longer the underdog, she loses what makes her someone to root for. "I shouldn't be, but I'm embarrassed about how you could tell my light was starting to fade at a certain point," she says. "I think that's because I took a lot of things on, and I just started getting angry and defensive. Like, this is my wall, and you won't break through it."

She hasn't been back on *The Challenge* since that tough loss. Taking a long break from the spotlight has helped her heal and find herself again, and she credits her boyfriend, Paulie, with helping her in her time away. "I am a boss for overcoming all of my circumstances," she says. "I don't like whiny baby victim Cara Maria, and I'm never going to be that girl again. When I became a boss, when I started winning, it's because I owned who I am. I like who I am now." But she also knows she needs to get back into the elimination ring again and rediscover the underdog that people love to root for. "I'm just in such a better place now, and I got that by taking my power back. I miss eliminations. I'm ready to win again. I'm ready to up that elimination record so nobody can touch it. Throw me in. Let me get my hands dirty. I'm ready to come back as a whole new good side of Cara that you loved with the strength of the Cara that I am now. You hear that, *Challenge* gods?"

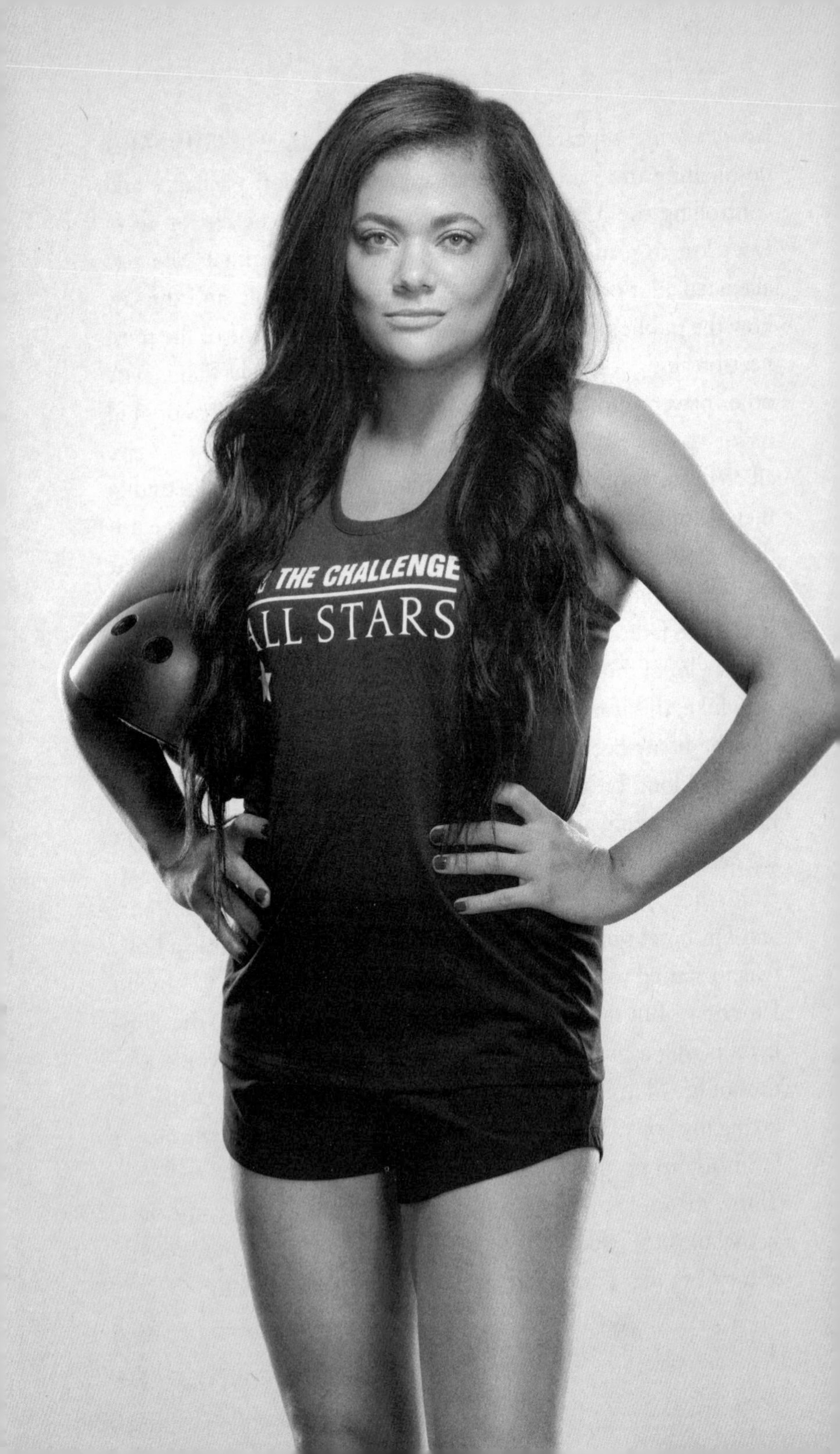
THE CHALLENGE
ALL STARS

JONNA MANNION

Champion: *All Stars 2, All Stars 3*

Most *Challenge* champions will tell you that winning takes a lot of heart. But for Jonna Mannion, playing with her heart got her nowhere in the game. It wasn't until she changed her strategy and approached *The Challenge* with her brain instead of her emotions that she finally became a *Challenge* champion. It wasn't an easy or quick journey—it took her five seasons plus a seven-year break from the franchise before she finally won for the first time, on *All Stars 2* with her partner, M.J. Garrett, and then she immediately won the next season all on her own on *All Stars 3*. But she wouldn't change a thing about her path to finally becoming a champ . . . even with the lows she experienced along the way.

Jonna's first official season was *Rivals* in 2011 shortly after her debut on *The Real World: Cancun*. But she was actually meant to begin her *Challenge* career on *Fresh Meat II* in 2010. Unfortunately, while at the airport the day the cast was flying to Canada to begin filming, she realized she'd lost her passport, so she had to turn around and go right back home. "I always think of that as my life was altered at that moment," she says.

"What would it have been like if I was on *Fresh Meat II*? What if I started out with all those relationships? But everything happens for a reason. Maybe I wasn't ready then. I was on *The Challenge* for so long, but it's only now I'm finally a champion. I think I was always meant to win *All Stars* instead."

After losing the last female elimination in her rookie season, Jonna competed on 2012's *Battle of the Seasons*, *Rivals II*, *Free Agents*, and *Battle of the Exes II*, but she never made a final in any of her attempts on the main franchise. She was always partying or caught up in some kind of relationship drama or on the wrong side of the house politics instead. She wasn't seen as a threat in eliminations and didn't have many daily challenge wins. Smash cut to a decade later on the first season of *All Stars*, and she entered the game as a whole new player. Jonna shifted her focus to the political side of the game, successfully avoided every single elimination, and made it to her first final. And despite being seven months postpartum and not having trained for the season at all, she tied for third place in the grueling final alongside KellyAnne Judd, getting beat only by the season's winner, Yes Duffy, and runner-up, Darrell Taylor. So what changed in her time away from *The Challenge* to turn her into a legitimate threat in the game?

It's actually a simple answer: she finally started taking the game seriously, both physically and mentally. On her original seasons, Jonna was in her early twenties and only cared about having a good time, which is why she always came up short in the actual competition. "I wasn't even thinking about the game. All of my first five *Challenge* seasons, I treated the whole experience like it was real life," she says. She saw the other cast members as her friends rather than her opponents and didn't want to risk hurting any "real" relationships she made on the show, which affected every single move she ever made (or didn't make). "I never really thought about *The Challenge* as a game to be won, with money as the ultimate goal. And that's the most growth that I've had from then until now; coming onto *All Stars*, I was able to separate it. I have my own life, I have a family, I have a husband—I grew up and became my own person, and I realized this is just a game. And I needed to play it to win."

She never forgot how three-time champion Jordan Wiseley once told her that someone like her could never win *The Challenge* because she was too good of a person; she'd never be good enough at the politics of the game. "He was right at the time—I never understood the political part of it," Jonna says. But she also wasn't given the chance to even try to work at that aspect of her game on her fifth season because of the way her partner treated her. "On *Battle of the Exes II*, I wasn't allowed to be a part of any of the politics because Zach [Nichols] was literally like, 'Don't talk to anybody about anything that has to do with the game. You're not allowed.' I always knew my self-worth and that I'm just as good as the other people here, but I was so worried about saying something that would make him upset or hurt someone's feelings, so I didn't stand up for myself." She regrets not challenging him in those moments and wishes she took more of an active role in the decision-making for their team. But she also admits that she wasn't the best partner to work with at the time, either. "I think it was a coping mechanism, but I would just shut down."

Jonna calls *Exes II* her lowest moment because of how she was treated by her partner and how she reacted to it, and it's a big reason why she didn't return to *The Challenge* for so long after it ended. "I feel like I left my *Challenge* career on a bad note," she says. "I was broken as a person, your partner was your ex, and with how things ended with me and him, it was just a toxic environment. Because of that, I decided that I didn't want to be a part of this anymore. So to be given the opportunity to come back on *All Stars* years later and rewrite my story and prove to myself and to the world that it was within me all along, it's just awesome. I finally found my voice. I don't know if that came with age or maybe being a mom and having two other lives depend on me, but now I trust myself and the decisions I make, in the game and in life. And that's what I needed to do all along."

When she was invited to join the cast of *All Stars* as a replacement for another player who had to drop out last-minute, she was excited to finally show the world what she could now accomplish on her own. There was just one problem—she only had two weeks' notice to prepare to reenter the *Challenge* world. She had just given birth to her son seven months earlier and wasn't in the shape she needed to be in to compete well. And she was completely out of practice in the social and political aspects of the game. So, she decided to take a back seat and follow her friend Jemmye Carroll's lead, and they both made it to the final that season. "I learned so much from watching her that season, so coming into *All Stars 2*, I understood more," Jonna says. "I was able to find a balance between still keeping my integrity as a good person but also playing smart. And it helped that I was underestimated because of my prior seasons. I wasn't seen as a big player, so that worked to my advantage."

And for the first time, Jonna trained prior to arriving at a *Challenge* season. "After *All Stars*, once I realized that there may be more shows, I was like, 'I don't know if I'll be asked, I don't know what's going to happen, but I'm just going to work my hardest to train because if the opportunity is presented, then I want to be prepared for it,'" she says. "I had just learned that the final isn't about who's physically the strongest—doing well in the final is about how mentally strong you are as well. Brute strength is good for eliminations and daily challenges and stuff like that, but in the final it's about endurance and your mental strength to carry on. It's mind over matter, and I needed to get better at that."

As soon as Jonna got back home after that first *All Stars* season, she got to work. She started doing heart rate–based high-intensity interval training (HIIT) workouts and running three miles every day. When she arrived in Mexico for *All Stars 2*, she scheduled all her workouts and runs to be at the hottest part of the day so she'd be acclimated to the elements. This time, she was going to be ready for anything. "Honestly, I can't even tell you how many crazy looks I got from people in the house, but I would run in the middle of the day when it was hot as hell and everybody's chilling in the pool or staying in the house to be cool," she says. "But I knew that if I'm there in the end, my body and my heart had to be ready. My mind's going to be ready because that's the hardest part."

And most importantly, Jonna spent the majority of time on *All Stars 2* making connections with everyone in the house and working the political side of the game. She found it easier than she expected to focus on the social dynamics of the house, because she's naturally a friendly person. But now the difference was, she forced herself to use that as a tool in the game and leveraged the connections she made to stay out of eliminations, especially the final one of the season. "It's not like I was being fake or doing it just for the game, but I finally understood how to use that side of things to my advantage," she says. What

Jonna (with M.J.) getting her first taste of victory during the
All Stars 2 final.

had once been a weakness was now a strength, as evidenced by
the fact that Jonna avoided every elimination that season. "The
final itself is really hard, but making it to the end, that's the
hardest part," she says. "And not going into a single elimination, it's more complicated than it seems. But there's so much
outside of your control in eliminations that you have a much
better chance at winning if you avoid going in completely. And
yeah, people are pissed about it, like, 'She didn't even earn this.
She didn't even have to go into elimination.' But making it to
the end without a single elimination is a whole art in itself, and
I feel like people don't appreciate that as much as they should."

Everything she had learned about herself from her previous
seasons helped her finally become a champion by the end of *All
Stars 2*. "I'll never forget the feeling of crossing the finish line
and realizing I won *The Challenge*. It was all worth it," she says.
And winning *The Challenge* brought out a new inner strength
that she took home into her daily life. "It instilled a new confidence in me. If I can run those finals, make it to the end, and

then also win, I literally feel like I can do anything. I feel like the world is at my fingertips now."

That's why she decided to return the next season for *All Stars 3*, but she had no idea that she was about to face her toughest—and most satisfying—season yet. Jonna entered the game as the reigning female champion, and with that title came a lot of pressure. But she more than lived up to it by delivering her best physical, social, and political performances ever, consistently finishing in the top during daily challenges, winning two eliminations, and even defending her reputation when Beth Stolarczyk entered the game as a replacement midway through the season and targeted Jonna by attacking her personal life.

"I was nervous, because there was a lot of drama and at one point I just wanted to go home," she says. "Beth literally said, 'I want to go against Jonna [in an elimination] because she's having an affair and cheating on her husband.' It had nothing to do with the game, she doesn't know me personally, it's just from a rumor she's heard, but I was sitting with a producer crying, saying, 'Go ahead and book my flight, I'm not even doing any exit interviews.' Just the emotional toll and stress I was feeling, it was rough. I signed up for this, obviously, but my husband didn't, my kids didn't, and the Internet lives forever. It felt like it was not worth it to me to be here, but I sure am glad I didn't quit."

For Jonna, quitting was never really an option, even when things got as difficult as they did on *All Stars 3*. She knew how hard she had worked to better herself as a *Challenge* competitor, and she wasn't going to let anyone ruin her chances at winning another season, especially when she was at the top of her game. "I stuck through it, and while I thought season two was the best because it was my first win, season three ended up being the best," Jonna says. "Season one, I figured out that it is possible for me to win because I came so close, and then I came back and got the win, but I was still learning even in season two. And season two, I relied on a partner, so season three, I stayed because there was something for me to prove, whether it's to the world or just myself: eliminations."

Before *All Stars 3*, Jonna's elimination record was only two wins out of seven, which is, to put it lightly, not great. She knew eliminations didn't play to her strengths, which is why she honed her social and political game during the first two seasons of *All Stars* to avoid them entirely. But the time had come to face what scared her the most. "The overall fear of going in is what drives a lot of people in the game, and people will go to any length to avoid it at all costs—I learned how to do that," she says. "Eliminations seemed like this big monster to me, and they're not. I realized that either I'd go home to my family and this stress could all be over, or I can prove myself and everyone else wrong and win."

And she did. Jonna forced herself to overcome her fear of eliminations and walked away with not one but two wins, sending both Beth and two-time champ Roni Martin-Chance home. "Winning an elimination gives you that confidence and that fire, like, 'Man, I just did that,'" she says. "I competed and I earned my spot here." And as an added bonus, winning those two eliminations gave her the leg up she needed to ultimately win the final by earning five points before the race even began, which ended up putting her in first place by the end. "I had self doubt. I wasn't sure if I could even do it. But that season is epic for me because I did win two eliminations and then also it came out as an individual win. In the end, I didn't rely on anybody except for myself. I didn't have any crutches of help with the political part or a partner or anything. It was all up to me this time, and I did it. Being alone is scary, but once you realize your capabilities, there's really no stopping you. Just knowing who I am now, standing on my own two feet, overcoming my own fears, and getting it done was big for me."

Proving to herself that she was a champ in her own right was her number one priority in returning for *All Stars 3*, but she also found herself being validated as a top *Challenge* competitor by some of the best in the game after they saw how she dominated that season. "When I got on the boat at the end of the final, T.J. makes such a big deal about me winning back-to-back and then [*All Stars 3* male winner] Wes [Bergmann] is like, 'Jonna, you're a way different player than ten years ago. You're one of the smartest people to ever play the game,'" she remembers. "And I was like, 'Wait, really? Coming from you, Mr. Thinks He's the Smartest Person?' And he says, 'Jonna, I think you're actually smarter than me.' I'm like, 'Did all the cameras catch all that?!' It was a full-circle moment because he was there at my first *Challenge* on *Rivals*, and to win next to somebody that's seen me evolve from the start was amazing."

All the highs and lows she experienced during *All Stars 3* further proved to Jonna that separating the game from real life is the real winning strategy. "It's just a game, and if you can play and take the emotions out of it, then you come out on top," she says. "Despite the BS that happened or almost happened, it's a happy ending to the story for me. I look at my life and the moment that I'm in right now is where I've always wanted to be. But if I've learned anything, it's just that I'm a badass. I really am. I'm a strong mom, and I'm glad that people finally have gotten to see me for who I truly am."

Now she's channeling all of that into being the parent for her two kids that she always wished she'd had. "I look at my little girl—I got put into the foster care system right at the age that she is now," Jonna says. "I feel like I'm looking at myself, but she has the family, the support, the love, the financial means, and a strong, confident mom and dad and family that is going to help her be the best person she can be."

Jonna also hopes that she can inspire other moms who have watched her journey on *The Challenge*, especially crossing the finish line on *All Stars* when she was still pumping her breast milk and reacclimating to life after giving birth. "I was a mess, literally, even more than what they showed," she says. "And it's been amazing to see how more and more moms are reaching out to me, saying things like, 'I cried when you crossed the finish line,' or, 'If you can do this, I can overcome postpartum depression.' I love knowing that I'm able to help others just by being me. I struggle most days. And I want to show how that's normal. You can still struggle but come out on top."

For now, Jonna is content to close the book on her *Challenge* experience. She doesn't plan on returning to compete again after winning back-to-back seasons of *All Stars*, because she doesn't think she has anything more to accomplish or prove to anyone. "I can't say no, but it's going to be a while until anybody sees me again," she says. "In my *Challenge* career, I'm at the very top. Not many people get the back-to-back wins, so I can't really go up from here. But hey, I'm still open. You never know what could happen in the future." Spoken like a true *Challenge* champ.

THE THREE-TIME CHAMPS

VERONICA PORTILLO

Champion: *Challenge 2000*, *The Gauntlet*, *The Inferno*

Whether you consider her to be a savvy political mastermind, a dominant physical player, or even a mean-girl bully, it doesn't matter—Veronica Portillo carved out her legacy as one of the best *Challenge* champions of all time long ago, and, as of this book's publication, no woman has ever done better than her. She made history as the first person to win three seasons of *The Challenge*, and that record has never been broken by another woman (only Evelyn Smith has since tied it). And what's even more impressive than Veronica's legendary resume is the fact that she built it by excelling in every aspect of the competition: her athletic performance, political savvy, and strong control of the social game.

Veronica's always had an analytical way of thinking, ever since she was a child. "It's just the way I'm wired," she says. "I've always looked at things a little differently than others. I like to find loopholes in rules and see things from an outsider's perspective." She never predicted that would end up benefiting her as much as it has on *The Challenge*, however. "I mean, you can't succeed in this game unless you're performing well, so my performance was always my number one focus, and then number two would be my political game. But on top of it all, I just always had a will to win."

That drive to succeed is actually the reason Veronica chose to continue with reality TV after her disastrous debut on *Road Rules: Semester at Sea* in 1999, where she spent much of the season fighting with her castmates. But she still said yes immediately when she was invited on *The Challenge* for season three, *Challenge 2000*, a few months later. "I left *Road Rules* with a pretty sour taste in my mouth—and a lot of it was my own fault—but I didn't want to end my time like that," she says. "I made myself go on *The Challenge* because I wanted to have a positive experience and rewrite my story."

At the time, she intended to do one season and then wrap up her reality TV career. But as soon as she arrived and met her new castmates, she could already tell that she was going to want to return again and again. "My original season of *Road Rules* just didn't mesh as a group, but on *The Challenge*, we all got along fantastically," she says. "It was so great. Everyone had the right attitude, and the camaraderie I was missing before was there. I just expected to be brought out of my comfort zone, try new things, and push my limits—all of which I did."

Veronica's *Road Rules* team won the majority of the challenges that season, but the one she remembers the most was the final mission, in which everyone had to solo skydive and land within a target for points. "This was my favorite challenge of all time," she says. "The competitions back then were different, but this was so scary. You had to jump alone. I was the last person on the plane that had to jump, and I remember thinking, 'Holy shit, I'm not going to be able to do this.' I talked myself into doing it as I was hyperventilating. My goggles were all fogging up." She remembers that the first two guys who jumped missed the target completely, but she was able to steer herself and land right in the middle. "A large reason why my team won was because I landed in the bullseye. The rush from the fear of failure and then coming out on top and being the only one who had landed in the bullseye is something that I'll never forget."

She remembers being so giddy when she finished that she could barely form words. "My teammate Dan [Setzler] rushed toward me and was like, 'You did so good!'" she says. "I just looked at him and was like, 'I'm amazing.' I couldn't say anything else. I didn't even mean to say that. But he just laughed at me and was like, 'Yeah, you are amazing.' It was nuts." She walked away that season a little bit richer and with a brand-new car, but more importantly with a new level of self-confidence she never expected. "I learned I'm a lot stronger than I give myself credit for, and that fear is just in the mind and that you could be your own biggest obstacle."

Veronica was thrilled when she was asked to come back for 2002's *Battle of the Seasons*. Unfortunately, after coming off such a meaningful victory, that experience couldn't have been more opposite. *Battle of the Seasons* introduced a new twist in which players could be voted out of the game, and Veronica and her partner, Yes Duffy, made history as the first two people ever to be eliminated from *The Challenge*. "God, that was so short-lived," she says with a laugh. "I had higher hopes and expectations for it, that it was going to mirror my experience on my first *Challenge*, that I was going to be able to push my limits and try new things and test my boundaries and all those things, and it literally lasted a couple days." She was more disappointed than anything that the new twist cut her game short, rather than being shocked by how the show evolved. "We knew that there were more people there than ever, and in the time between *Challenge 2000* and *Battle of the Seasons*, shows like *Survivor* had premiered and changed the landscape of our show. We influenced *Survivor*, then they influenced us to make it more exciting."

When she returned for the next season, *Battle of the Sexes*, Veronica was once again voted out by her own team and realized that her strategy had to change along with the show. "At first, it was a fun game where we all just got along and worked together as a team to achieve a common goal," she says. "And then having your team members eliminate you because you did well and were considered a threat to them, that didn't sit right with me. I knew going back that, in order to survive and succeed in the game, I was going to have to play unfairly. I was going to have to play for myself. It brought out a little fighter in me."

Veronica came back with a vengeance the next season. She decided there was no way she was getting eliminated from *The Gauntlet*, and she just had to figure out a way to make the game work for her. "I started looking at things much differently, analyzing the rules and thinking of all types of loopholes and ways to be able to beat the game," she says. "I felt like I had been cheated out of the last two seasons, so I wasn't going to play nice anymore. I realized that's just the way the game is supposed to be played—you can either play the game or have the game play you."

On *The Gauntlet*, everyone understood that a team is only as strong as its weakest player, and Veronica continued to perform well in the daily challenges to keep herself safe. Her name still ended up on the chopping block, however, after her teammate Sarah Greyson went into five eliminations. "There were two times where it was like, 'In order to be fair, it's Veronica's turn to go in,' so my ass was on the line because people were starting to feel bad for Sarah," Veronica says. But both times, Veronica won first place in the challenge, earning the Lifesaver when she needed it most. "I was able to get myself out of trouble, and I didn't have to do it politically—I competed my way out of it."

While her athletic performance saved her that season, she learned that she still needed to have a strong political game as backup. "Rachel [Robinson] has a very good political game that no one ever saw, and she definitely coached me a lot," Veronica says. "I think that she's actually the meaner one of the two of us, although I get the heat for it." As Veronica became more cutthroat to survive at the expense of other players, she didn't care that it earned her the reputation of being a mean girl or a bully if it meant that she was safe. "It sounds cruel and evil, but I didn't struggle with that, because I had this 'win at all costs' mentality. In fact, I felt like those were the rules of the game: We want to keep our strongest on the team, so why would we sacrifice a stronger competitor over a weaker player?"

However, there was a fine line to walk between playing an ironclad political game and still making sure her social game didn't suffer too much as a result. "The hardest obstacle I had to overcome was probably the preconceived notion that I was just a bitch," she says. "There's a part of me that's pretty shy and insecure, and it takes me a while to open up with new people. I'm not the best at first impressions, so usually people dislike me before they like me. I had to work really hard at making myself likable or changing their minds about who they thought I was from my edit on television. As a result, being on *The Challenge* gave me the confidence that I was lacking and made me more outgoing. A lot of those walls just broke down. To win *The Challenge*, I think you have to push your pride to the side sometimes and figure out how you can become a better person."

Her hard work paid off that season when she made it to the final with her *Road Rules* team. Unlike her rookie season, this final challenge was more of a marathon, but the thought of giving up never once crossed her mind. "It was like a modern-day final," she remembers. "We ran, like, seven and a half miles through crazy terrain at a very high elevation in Telluride, Colorado, so the oxygen was very thin. It was brutal." The struggle made her team's eventual win that much sweeter, and when she got home with her second *Challenge* championship, her confidence went through the roof. "I felt unstoppable. It really boosted my self-esteem and ego. I found myself taking more risks—I used to have my whole life planned, every little detail, and I became a lot more spontaneous. It was totally freeing. *The Challenge* completely changed my attitude toward life and people and my willingness to do things and my lack of fear, which has been a very nice blessing."

Now a two-time champ, Veronica was hooked on *The Challenge* and couldn't wait to return for *The Inferno* the next season. "It became a drug that I was addicted to," she says with

Veronica's not afraid to get down and dirty for the win.

a laugh. "The things that we got to do were just so crazy and fun. My expectations for life were a lot higher. You're not necessarily satisfied with normalcy. I knew winning was possible, and I knew that I was competitively one of the best females, so I went in with an attitude that I can win, and I was going to win again. There was nothing that was going to stop me." She used everything she learned from her past experiences to hone her physical, political, and social strategy and made it to another final without seeing a single elimination. She won her third championship on *The Inferno*, making her the first competitor ever to achieve this feat.

But Veronica hasn't won again after returning for six more seasons on the main franchise—*Battle of the Sexes 2, The Inferno II, The Ruins, XXX: Dirty 30, Vendettas,* and *Final Reckoning*—as well as stints on the *Champs vs. Pros* and *All Stars* spin-offs. She thinks she'd have more wins by now if she had continued her trajectory of competing every single season—she was even offered the opportunity to be the first real "face" of *The Challenge* by doing that—but she made the conscious decision to take breaks from the show instead after *The Inferno II* in 2005 because of a disagreement with the producers. "I didn't know when the calls would stop coming, so I felt like I had very little control of my livelihood," she says. "I thought it was really important to get something going outside of the *Challenge* world." That's why Veronica and Rachel created the 2000s College Dropout T-shirt line as a side hustle. Since *The Challenge* didn't have a formal uniform for the competitors at the time, everyone wore shirts from their line on *The Inferno II*, which served as free publicity for the company. "When they were casting the following season, they told me that they wanted me back, but that my T-shirts were not allowed. I felt like the show wasn't necessarily supporting the endeavor we did on the side and helping that grow. I got angry that I couldn't represent my T-shirt brand on the show, so that's the reason why I walked away, which is crazy to think about now."

Still, Veronica will always be proud of how *The Challenge* helped her grow as a person. "The path that my life took was only because of *The Challenge*, so in a big way, I feel like all my successes are due to that," she says. She currently works in sales, and her time on *The Challenge* taught her everything she needed to know to do well in her current job. "It shaped me into who I am and how I approach things. If I fall down, I pick myself right back up and I keep going. I don't let self-doubt win. And I don't let the opinions other people have of me affect me. I'd probably be living a very, very ordinary life if it wasn't for *The Challenge*."

JORDAN WISELEY

Champion: *Battle of the Exes II, XXX: Dirty 30, War of the Worlds 2*

If Jordan Wiseley had never won *The Challenge*, his life would be completely different today. He'd still be in his Oklahoma hometown, either running his father's construction company or starting his own with friends. He'd be dreaming about the life he'd always wanted—to live in Los Angeles and become an actor—but he wouldn't have any idea how to make that a reality. It's thanks to the money from his first win, *Battle of the Exes II* in 2014 with his partner, Sarah Rice, that he was able to move to Los Angeles and start his acting career, achieving one dream that then made the other possible. Later, he would return to *The Challenge* to win two more seasons in a row. It sounds like the picture-perfect, life-changing *Challenge* journey, doesn't it?

Life-changing, it certainly was. But Jordan's path toward getting his first, second, and third wins was anything but perfect. He made a lot of mistakes and had to learn some hard lessons along the way to grow both as a *Challenge* competitor and as a person. It all began on his rookie season, *Rivals II* in

2013. He had been invited on *The Challenge* only a month after he got home from filming *The Real World: Portland*, and he was already in Thailand filming *Rivals II* when *The Real World: Portland* premiered. "That was nuts because our show hadn't come out yet," Jordan says. "I wasn't on social media or anything for the first two months of me being on TV; I wasn't even in society. I would walk into interviews for *Rivals II* and the producers would be like, 'Hey, just so you know, episode three [of *The Real World*] is starting to air right now in the States. I'm like, 'Cool. I wish I could watch it.'"

The morning after he and his *Rivals II* partner and *Real World: Portland* castmate, Marlon Williams, came in third place and were cut on the first day of the final, they were finally able to check the Internet on the hotel computers. Everything hit them all at once—the good, the bad, and the ugly of public opinion from their reality TV debut. Suffice to say, it was a lot to handle. "The love and the hate and the backlash, I got it all," Jordan says. "It was just a dumping of everything. I went back to my room shell-shocked."

At the time, Jordan was twenty-two, an age when most people are still figuring themselves and their futures out. The response to his actions and personality on *The Real World* combined with how his season unfolded on *Rivals II* was like a self-help therapy crash course as he watched himself get into fights that he ultimately regretted. "It informed me a lot about myself," he says. "You see yourself and you're like, wow, do I do that? Do I talk like that? Do I cut people off like that? Definitely, for me, it was like, you've got some work to do."

On *The Challenge*, he had been treating the competition purely like sports, which he had grown up playing with an inferiority complex due to his being born with only one hand. He always felt like he had something to prove as a result: "In my mind, I can't just do what they do. I have to do it better. It has to be spectacular, because there has to be a reason why they're going to go with the guy with only one hand who technically is a bigger risk. And this was all the way from a young age to college sports."

As a result, he had a tendency to compete aggressively, often with a chip on his shoulder. But he didn't anticipate that the other competitors on *The Challenge* would perceive that negatively. "I flip a switch mentally when I'm competing, and that rubbed people the wrong way," he says. "Nobody likes arrogance, but for me, that was a survival technique that I was using my whole life. I had the need to show that I am the best all-around athlete to ever grace this show." Seeing that approach captured on camera on *Rivals II* made him realize that was his biggest insecurity. "We found out that I can't be not good at something, and I've had to learn when to dial that back. I did well that season because I competed well, but it caused a tougher political and social journey. I learned that I had to assess myself and put a bigger focus on the social and political side of the game, more so than the physical game. Basically, I had to get better at being a good person."

That epiphany set him up well for his next season on *Free Agents* in 2014. But this time, he took it too far in the other direction. "I was like, 'I got it now, I know how this game works,' and I was much better at the social game. But I used my powers for evil instead of for good or self-preservation," he says. He built strong alliances but went on a power trip as a result, knowing he had the numbers on his side, which culminated in his own demise halfway through the season during the infamous Wrecking Wall elimination against Johnny "Bananas" Devenanzio. "I was doing so well socially, we got them all to vote in Johnny Bananas, and then I threw myself in against him and lost," he says.

He had nothing to blame but his own ego for losing the chance at making another final. "It was stupid; I could have walked to that final on *Free Agents* because I had the support of the house, and Laurel Stucky and I were together and she was running the house as well," he says. It was yet another eye-opening lesson he had to learn, about both the game and his own personality. "I realized you don't get paid to win eliminations or stupid little victories of, like, winning an argument," he says. "You only get paid to win the whole thing. Keep your eye on the prize, buddy."

When he returned for his third season, it was with a new focus and a better understanding of how to communicate with and treat people. "I went too far left on season one, I went too far right on season two, and then season three, I found that happy medium. For me, the best way to play the mental game is not playing their game," Jordan says. "I don't do Twitter beefs and I don't do online drama. You can say whatever you want about me, but I'm just about the game. That's where it goes down. Now I try to just go with the flow."

He worked hard on keeping his emotions and pride in check, which wasn't easy in that high-stakes atmosphere. "It doesn't matter if it's your first elimination or your tenth, your heart is racing no matter what," he says. "But the secret is you can't show it. You've got to walk around with your head up, like it's just another day. Go put on a good show and ride off in the sunset with a good elimination highlight if you lose or you win."

And for someone who previously wouldn't allow himself to be anything but the best, Jordan had to learn his hardest lesson yet. "You have to be okay with failing," he says. "If you want to get somewhere cool, somewhere worth getting, you have to get rid of that fear of failure. And that's really how I play *The Challenge* now and live my life. Don't be scared to go for it. If you want to make it to the final, you've got to be willing to risk some ego, some pride, and keep the bigger picture in mind. You don't get anything out of winning an argument with somebody."

It took three seasons of working on bettering himself for Jordan to finally win *The Challenge* on *Battle of the Exes II.*

XXX: Dirty 30 was leaps and bounds one of Jordan's best seasons.

He knows he couldn't have done it without every single lesson he learned along the way. His reward was not only earning the long-coveted title of *Challenge* champion and the cash prize that came with it, but also getting to experience his first full final, which he realized is his favorite part about competing. "What interests me the most about *The Challenge* are the finals—I want to go long and fast, I want to kayak, I want to swim, I want to bike, I want to pick up a bunch of shit, and I want to do it in cool places," he says. "I loved every minute of the *Exes II* final in Norway. We jumped out of helicopters. I don't even mind eating all the stupid crap. We got to climb a mountain, then we stayed up all night to finish day two. The cold sucked, but it's such a test. Maybe these are the kind of people you call sick, but I want to know what I can do!"

That's why you'll never see him complaining during a final, not even when he starts it off with what should have been a season-ending injury. On Jordan's next season, *XXX: Dirty 30* in 2017, he once again used all his prior knowledge and experience to make it to the final, which began with every player skydiving out of a plane. Even though they were all strapped to professionals, Jordan crash-landed and instantly knew something was wrong with his leg.

"I'm not going to lie, for the first fifteen minutes after hitting the ground, I was like, 'My legs are fucking broken,'" he says. "We jumped from eighteen thousand feet, and it's a chilly Argentinian morning out in the desert, and then we jump from that altitude, so it's cold, and when you're cold, everything hurts worse. When we slammed, my feet went numb, and I couldn't move them. My shins felt the same way. And I was like, 'This is really, really bad.'"

He was taken directly to an ambulance to get checked out. He was panicking, thinking his final was over before it even began. But he refused to let his season end this way despite being in excruciating pain, because the word "quit" just isn't in his vocabulary. He jumped out of the ambulance and started to just walk around to see if his body could handle continuing. "I've been hurt a lot growing up: I had multiple surgeries on each knee, my elbow has been reconstructed," he says. "I raced motocross, did rodeos. We grew up in the country and played rough, so I've been in that situation before, having to assess: Are you hurt or are you injured? If you're just hurt, you can get up and keep going. But if you're injured, we're going to call somebody."

Against medical advice, Jordan decided that he was just hurt and not injured, and he was going to continue running the final. "In my mind, all I could think about during the rest of it was, if you win this, it'll be so freaking cool," he says. And despite having a fracture on the inside of his upper tibia, he continued to the first checkpoint—only to discover it required running up and down a hill full of boulders and holes, carrying heavy rocks. For someone pushing through a lot of pain in his legs already, he thought he had no chance at winning now. But he still didn't let himself quit, and that determination paid off. He finished that checkpoint in first place, which gave him the boost of confidence he needed to continue on and ultimately win the whole thing. "That should have been my weakest event, really, and I ended up inching it out, and that's another lesson I learned: find the little wins," he says. "Don't ever be discouraged, because you never know what's going to happen. At that point, I knew there was no way I was letting anyone else catch up."

Winning *XXX: Dirty 30* on an injured leg was a big victory for Jordan as he earned his second *Challenge* championship. But he was still learning some hard truths about himself. Earlier that season, he made an offensive joke to his friend Jemmye Carroll on a night out, saying she had a "Down syndrome face." He knew immediately he'd crossed a line back then, and looking back on that moment now, it's one of his biggest regrets. "That's not how I feel as someone who's been very, very close to the disabled community my entire life," he says. "And I've always been close with Jemmye so it sucked to hurt her feelings. The alcohol was flowing and you think something's funny in the moment, but it was not funny."

As a result of that night, Jordan decided to cut back on his drinking. But the bigger takeaway is that he pays more attention to what he says and how he talks to others, both on and off the show. "Dealing with people from all walks of life on *The Challenge* has taught me how to communicate with others and that not everybody communicates the way that you do," he says. "I know my intention when I'm telling someone something, but it could come off in another way, so I've had to learn to see things from other people's perspectives."

And he knows that actions speak louder than words, so on the show and in real life, he works every day to prove that he's listening and learning from all his mistakes. "People mess up, but it's how you act afterwards that is your character," he says. "If you made a mistake, own up to it. You don't keep making that mistake, because then it's not a mistake; that's a habit. You have to take a hard look at yourself and see, Where does this come from? And how can I fix it?"

That's part of the reason why he took a four-season break from *The Challenge* after his first win, and then again after

XXX: Dirty 30. Both times, he wanted to decompress, do some soul-searching, and work on himself—as well as lessen the target on his back as a *Challenge* threat. He doesn't regret turning down the offer to go on two other seasons, including *Battle of the Bloodlines* in 2015 with his younger brother (who Jordan says is even more athletic than he is), because he needed the time away. He even turned down the invitation to join *XXX: Dirty 30* initially, because at the time, his acting career was taking off (he had a recurring role on Tyler Perry's *If Loving You Is Wrong*). But MTV and Bunim/Murray Productions convinced him that this was one he didn't want to miss, and they were right—he would go on to win half a million dollars and secure his second championship that season.

From checking his ego to learning how to better communicate with others to not fearing failure, everything that Jordan's learned on *The Challenge* has also helped him off the show in his personal and professional relationships. But what he values most now is integrity. "If you say you're going to do something, do it; if you say you're not going to do something, you'd better not do it," he says. "I don't care how much pressure gets put on you, you've got to stick to that. I've never made a backdoor deal with anybody, I've never gone back on a decision or a handshake, and I want to be able to stand by that in real life. I want to be known as the guy you can trust."

It's why Jordan's third win, on 2019's *War of the Worlds 2*, is the most meaningful to him. He felt like he and his then fiancée, Tori Deal, were battling all season long against the "bullies" on Team USA, who weren't sticking to their word or practicing team loyalty. After Jordan and Tori were both thrown into elimination, they became turncoats and defected to Team UK, who ended up winning in the final. "I just love the story of it: Team USA is so dominant and then they cannibalize and fall apart. They had all this power and then get smashed at the end," he says as he smiles. "You guys were the bullies and then we beat you. It really felt like against all odds, because we had no control, and they were so smug about it."

Going through that experience gave Jordan an even greater appreciation for loyalty and integrity, and he now puts that into practice in his professional life every day. He owns a clothing company and always pays his manufacturers and fabric suppliers 100 percent of the costs up front for big orders, rather than following the industry standard of paying partially in advance and the rest when the order is fulfilled. It shocked the companies he did business with at first because it was unheard of, but it also created an instant bond of total trust, which led to even more success. "I ended up becoming an investor in two of the factories that we use now, because I stuck to what I said I was going to do, and it built this trust that goes both ways," he says. "It's an integrity thing. It's a loyalty thing. Do good by your people and they'll do good by you."

And it's all come full circle. After a three-year break, Jordan returned to the franchise for *All Stars 3* in 2022, and all the work he had done on bettering himself over his *Challenge* career paid off. Walking back into the *Challenge* world, he was worried about reintegrating with all the players. But his reputation preceded him. "It was actually pretty amazing, all these vets and all these people were coming up to me and they were like, 'We see how you play, and we just want to salute that because nobody does that,'" Jordan says. "That was pretty baller. That means a lot because that is what I want to be known for. Not that I have the most daily wins or elimination victories or championships, but that I played the best game that people respect and I'm living my best life."

It's been a long road to get here and it wasn't always pretty, but after six seasons and three championships, Jordan's evolution as a *Challenge* competitor and person is his biggest prize.

DERRICK KOSINSKI

Champion: *The Inferno 3, The Island, The Ruins*

Derrick Kosinski always has the odds stacked against him. At five feet seven inches, he's usually the smallest guy on the cast. He knows he'll never be the biggest, strongest, fastest, or even smartest (he'll be the first to tell you all about his lack of puzzle skills). But instead of letting the things that he can't control or change hold him back, he has found a way to become one of the best *Challenge* players of all time. How? By being the best teammate he can be.

It's a strategy he's been using his entire life, but he never realized how important it would be on *The Challenge*. Before Derrick got his start on reality TV, he was going to a community college outside of Chicago and playing basketball and baseball. He knew his size and athletic limitations but still found a way to excel in spite of them. "I was on a college baseball team that had major league talent—I was nowhere near the caliber of these dudes," Derrick says. "So, I did the little things: I bunted for base hits, I stole bases, I dove for balls, and I was the next guy up who basically could do it all. And when you compare

The Challenge, I'm still not the best at everything. But my base always came back to me being one of the best team players."

He's not exaggerating, and his *Challenge* resume proves it. After competing on five seasons, Derrick finally won his first *Challenge* on *The Inferno 3*, which was a team format. He then went on to win his next two seasons—*The Island* and *The Ruins*—which were also played in teams. "I've won three *Challenge* championships in a row with teams, so I don't call myself an individual champ," he says. "I'm a three-time team *Challenge* champ, and I take pride in that."

It took him a while to get to that point, however. After seeing an ad for auditions on TV, Derrick submitted a tape and was cast on *Road Rules: X-Treme* in 2004, which took him to Argentina and Chile. Back then, his mentality was simply, "I want to do awesomeness all the time." For him, that meant going on adventures that he'd never get the chance to do in his normal life, partying with people he'd never have met otherwise, and doing whatever seemed like the most fun thing in the moment. That approach served him well on *Road Rules* . . . but not on *The Challenge*. "My 'awesomeness all the time' attitude got me kicked out of the game pretty early."

Derrick got the call to join *The Challenge* for *Battle of the Sexes 2* in Santa Fe, New Mexico, just a few months after he finished *Road Rules: X-Treme*. He's the first to admit his rookie season was . . . well, terrible. "It was weird," he says. "I was homesick. I was not getting along with people in the house. My expectation on the show was to just do what I'd been doing for years, which was enjoying myself and competing. I played sports my whole life just because I love it, and now they're paying me to do it *and* do the partying thing? I was like, 'Fuck yeah!'"

But he realized very quickly that *The Challenge* was not *Road Rules*. "I walked in and was like, 'Man, let's fucking party,'" he says. "I brought a beer bong, a vodka bottle, ready to take shots, and these guys all looked at me like, 'Who the fuck is this?'" The party had definitely ended, and Derrick was in for a brutal wake-up call. "I was like, 'Hold on, man. I'm pretty sure I saw you, you, you, you, and you partying like this on all these *Real World* seasons; is this not what you guys do?' And they were like, 'Bam, perfect. This is the guy we want to take out of the game.'" That was Derrick's first realization that *Challenge* competitors look for any reason or excuse to vote someone out of the game or into elimination. In this case, he stuck out from the crowd and didn't work with the group as a whole, prioritizing partying and having a good time over focusing on the game, so the target was on him.

Derrick was the fifth guy voted out on *Battle of the Sexes 2*, and he still harbors a grudge against his former *Road Rules* castmate Nick Haggart because of it. "I believe it was Nick who said something like, 'Derrick's blunt. He's loud. He's brash,'" he says. "I didn't really know that this was going to come off as the hate-orade train. I did well in the competitions, and they still found a way to vote me off early." It took him some time to process that, despite his solid physical performance, the social and political aspects of the game were just as important—and he had completely ignored that.

His early exit on that first season haunted him. "I was banged up. I didn't realize that I can seemingly make all these friends and then all at one time, they're just like, get this guy out of here," he says. "That's the part of the game that I didn't know, and it was a mindfuck." He thought he was being a good teammate by performing well in the challenges and creating a fun vibe in the house, but he was betrayed by those he thought he could trust. That rude awakening opened his eyes to what *The Challenge* really is and how he needed to change his approach. As an athlete, he could always count on his teammates to have his back. But on *The Challenge*, he had to know when to stay loyal . . . and when to stab an ally in the back.

After his experience on *Battle of the Sexes 2*, Derrick knew he had to change his game if he wanted to stay longer. When he returned for the next season, *The Inferno II* in 2005, he remembered everything that he had learned from his rookie season. "That starts with relationships and good teammates and a good team," he says, now able to make the connection from his lifelong experiences as a reliable team player to *The Challenge*, a game he originally thought to be completely individual. "I kind of started seeing how things worked, and it was basically: you've got to have an alliance. You've got to have a group of people that you trust and that you make moves with, and you make these moves from different directions."

Derrick sure knew how to pick 'em for his first alliance. "On *Inferno II*, Darrell [Taylor] and C.T. [Tamburello] took me under their wing; we had the same vibe and just clicked," he says. "And me and Brad [Fiorenza] had already been on *Battle of the Sexes 2* together, and we were from the Chicagoland area so we had this rapport."

Not only did Derrick pick strong allies for his first-ever alliance, but he also strategically made sure they covered different areas of the game. "C.T. was on the Bad Asses team with me, and Darrell and Brad were on the Good Guys team on the other end, so this is the first time I saw the game being run like the mob," he says. "Call it whatever you want to call it, call it a strong alliance, but this is what you see in mobster movies, right? 'Who are we going to clip next? How are we going to do it?' We'd be in the bathroom while taking a piss, like, 'Who we gonna vote next?' That's the first time I saw how you have to attack this game from different angles to win."

And it worked much better this time around. Derrick made it all the way to the end of the season, competed in the final . . . and lost. "Darrell won with two other guys and Jamie Chung. We seemingly had the right strategy and put the right people in against each other to keep our numbers to our side," he says. But it ultimately didn't matter. This was yet another pivotal lesson that Derrick had to learn: you can't win them all. "The final was four of them versus seven of us, which hypothetically you would think we have more people, we'll probably do better," he says. "But no." He saw how having more people can actually be a disadvantage sometimes, depending on the task and who your teammates are, because your team is only as fast as its slowest runner. But sometimes more people *can* be the secret advantage you need to win—and there's no way to predict when that will happen. That's when he got a healthy appreciation for how luck can also be a big factor on *The Challenge*, and accepting that fact is much easier than fighting against it. "It's one of the things that people don't talk about. It's the X factor to success on *The Challenge* and in life: Sometimes the luck is on your side. But sometimes it's not."

And for a long time, luck was not on Derrick's side. But he still refused to give up hope. He had a run of frustrating close calls for his next three seasons. On *The Gauntlet 2*, Derrick fought and won four eliminations against massive heavy hitters, guys like Syrus Yarbrough and Brad who were twice his size. That's when he first started making a name for himself as the elimination underdog. "The Syrus battle—I've had conversations with him and he literally said, 'I thought I broke your neck. I don't know how your head stayed on your body.'" But despite his many hard-fought victories that season, he was still sent into the last men's elimination before the final and lost, which he says feels even worse than getting sent home first. On *Fresh Meat*, Derrick made it all the way through the season with his partner, Diem Brown, only to lose once again in the final elimination (against that season's winners, Darrell Taylor and Aviv Bruno [formerly Melmed]). The next season on *The Duel*, Derrick beat Tyler Duckworth in an elimination but ended up in another one and lost, once again, to that season's winner (Wes Bergmann) halfway through.

When he returned for *The Inferno 3*, his sixth season in a row, he had reached his make-it-or-break-it point. Derrick had been determined to stick with it—he'd had some good runs and could almost taste the win. The odds had to finally be in his favor, right? But the game was starting to take a toll on his confidence. "I was just like, man, if I don't win this, I'm going to be the biggest fucking loser," he says. "It was just, like, the most do-or-die. But if I die in this Inferno, I'm going to be fucked up forever because I've been trying to win this shit for five, six years."

He was once again sent into the final men's elimination, against yet another bigger guy, Davis Mallory. "I get another physical elimination against a slightly bigger guy who has a little bit of a football background, and I ended up beating him," he says. "It was just so amazing. And that was probably the worst shape I've ever been in, too." With this elimination win, he broke his streak and made it to another final. And thankfully, this time, the teams were even. "Somehow we pull this thing off, and I win my first *Challenge* championship," he says.

In looking back at what finally got him his first win, he credits how he'd built up his reputation as a reliable team player who could be trusted in an alliance and had proven himself time and time again in brutal, knock-down, drag-out elimination battles. "I think I finally gained the respect from my peers, like, 'I need this guy on my team,' and, 'I don't want to go against him because he might just bite my face off,'" he says with a laugh. "I paid my dues and people didn't want to fuck with me." He laughs again. "I got lucky to be on a cast that had people who wanted me on their team, who saw that team player in me, [someone] they felt like they needed at the end of this, who they can make moves with, who they trusted, and who would lay on the sword if they needed him to. It was that accompanied with just playing a smart game."

Now Derrick knew how to play the game. He built long-lasting relationships that could get him to the end. He finally had the winning record to match his reputation. So he ran with it. Derrick won his next two seasons by once again being the best teammate he could be and continuing to cultivate his alliances. He didn't stay completely out of the drama as much as he would have liked, but he also understood that you can't play a "squeaky clean game" and still win. "If you make it to the end, you've probably made a dirty, shady move," he says. "Every move is going to hurt somebody or affect somebody in a negative way, and it's either done by you, happening to you, or you're a bystander that sees it."

And when making a move against someone else, Derrick also knew from very early on that managing those hurt feelings is also important. "This ain't like *Big Brother*. This ain't like *Survivor*," he says. "I will probably see you next season, you're going to remember what I did, and we're going to have to figure out a way to work through this. But sometimes that bridge is burned, and it's going to be painful." Like the time he had to vote his *Road Rules: X-Treme* castmate Ibis Nieves into elimination on *The Ruins*. "I knew that this is where the cutthroat mentality comes into play," he says. "I have to do what's best for our team. I have to do what's best for me." And it ultimately was the right move because, once again, that good-team-player reputation saved him. When it was the final men's elimination on *The Ruins*, Johnny "Bananas" Devenanzio was chosen to go in instead of Derrick. "Somehow, Johnny created himself to be a bigger asshole [than me]. And then we had to come up with a way to explain it to him, like, 'It's your turn to go in an elimination, bro. Go get your feet wet. We've protected you the whole way here. Go take Dunbar [Merrill] out.' If you can't beat Dunbar, you shouldn't be going to the final anyway."

Now with three *Challenge* championships to his name—something that only five other players have ever achieved in the history of the franchise—Derrick's best moment still had yet to come. After competing on *Cutthroat* (and once again getting sent home in the final men's elimination), he wasn't back on *The Challenge* until *XXX: Dirty 30*. "The *Challenge* gods put me on the sideline for seven years," he says. In that time, Derrick had gotten divorced and was still coming to terms with his new normal. "They asked me to come back, and they know that the animal's ready to come out. But the animal really didn't know how to even, like, deal with civilization and society, let alone a fucking game where there's bombs going off everywhere."

Despite the long break, Derrick came back in full force and finished the season in second place, beating C.T. in the final and Johnny in an earlier elimination. It may not be the fourth championship he wanted (thanks to that puzzle in the final), but he was still proud for how he was able to take out *Challenge* legends along the way. And he was ready to do it again when he got the call to return as an alternate for *Vendettas*. But he wasn't needed in the game and was sent home without getting to compete.

The *Challenge* gods weren't done with him yet, though. And he was about to prove once again why he's one of the toughest elimination opponents of all time. Later that season on *Vendettas*, he was brought back as a Mercenary—all he had to do was compete in one elimination. There was nothing on the line except bragging rights. His opponent, Joss Mooney, however, was fighting for his life—both in the game and liter-

Derrick and the bane of his existence: a puzzle.

ally, because the physical battle between these two men became muddy, bloody, and brutal. "What's the best elimination of all time? People like the Bananas Backpack, but it's the Joss and Derrick elimination," he says. "I don't care what they say about the Johnny Bananas Backpack, which took nineteen seconds; it'll never compare to the ninety-minute war that me and this fucking British god went through on that day in Spain."

The elimination, Crazy 8, involved them wrestling with a figure eight–shaped ring in the pit. And once again, Derrick didn't let the massive size difference between him and Joss stop him. Both men attacked each other for an hour and a half in a war of attrition. "The adrenaline is through the roof— it was just two dudes beating the shit out of each other," he says. "Boxing matches don't go for ninety minutes. UFC fights do not go for ninety minutes. On TV, it says we went twelve rounds, but this thing went maybe a hundred fucking rounds."

It seemed like it would never end, but neither Derrick nor Joss was giving up. For Joss, it was understandable why he was killing himself in the ring—his spot in the game depended on it. But for Derrick, this was purely just for the love of good competition and putting on one hell of a show. "They stopped it at some point because I was split open and bleeding pretty badly," Derrick says. "They've got the flashlights out, three doctors, and they're like, 'They want to stitch you up. Do you want to keep going?' Do I want to keep going?! Don't you dare stop this at this point."

Derrick didn't care about the cut or the blood or getting stitches. He didn't care about how exhausted or beat up he was. All he wanted was to get right back in that ring and keep going. "And Joss tore his bicep, so when I got back in the ring, I'm like, 'Is that motherfucker getting medical attention, too? Hell yeah!'" he says. "We came back in and he gave one more huge fucking pull as hard as he can, everything he had, dragged me out of the ring, I just barely hold on. And then that was it for him. I could tell the next couple of rounds, I stood up and I controlled it."

The elimination finally ended on what seemed like a mental slip-up from Joss. He thought Derrick went out of bounds, so he turned his back to Derrick, believing the round was being reset. But Derrick says he actually faked it to throw Joss off. "When they say he had a mind lapse or whatever, no," he says. "I faked it, I stayed in bounds, and I went for it. [I think] it's because he lost all the control; he gave it his last ounce of energy and did not want to hit the ground again."

Derrick considers that Mercenary performance to be one of his proudest moments on *The Challenge*. "There will never be another elimination that long, that barbaric, that high-flying—the combat in that was fun and different," he says. "These eliminations against these bigger guys and the wars that I've been in set me apart from the rest. Before that Joss elimination, I already had a reputation of being one of the best at eliminations, one of the most hard-core if not the most hard-core. Like if there's a hard-core belt, I feel like I would have owned it for a very long time, and I think that put the stamp on it."

But when it comes to his all-time favorite moment from his *Challenge* career? "There's nothing like getting that first championship. Some people get it sooner than others, but for me, that was my sixth try," he says. By not giving up and finally winning for the first time, it proved that his hard work and dedication paid off. "For me, getting that first one, getting that monkey off your back, is my number one moment," he says. And becoming a *Challenge* champion had an unexpected benefit in his life, one he found to be priceless (which is ironic, considering it was made possible because of the cash prize): winning *The Challenge* allowed him to be the best father he could be. With his earnings, he was able to be home with his son, where he was able to pass down everything he'd learned about being a good teammate and trustworthy person. "For those first two years of his life, I was able to wake up with my son, be there with him, hold him like my little football, and not have to go to work every day and not see my kid," he says. "I was there from the moment he was born, and I was able to do it because of the *Island* and *Ruins* victories, and I won because I knew how to build those relationships and treated people with respect."

And now Derrick is continuing to use what he learned from *The Challenge* to make his *Challenge Mania* podcast a success. "The *Challenge Mania* podcast is doing better than ever; we're doing live shows at comedy clubs every other month, we've built a community, and it's all based on teamwork," he says. "It's a whole team of people behind the scenes, my cohost, Scott [Yager], and the fans who tune in and come to these live shows. And my son is able to see his dad having this really weird but interesting job that pays the bills thanks to this whole community behind us, because of my success, because of those elimination wins, losses, wars, three *Challenge* championships, arguably being one of the best that's ever done this thing. It's all been such a blessing that comes down to teamwork, respect, gratitude, work ethic."

He pauses before adding, "And putting on a good show. It took me a long time to realize that we have to put on a show. It's not just a sport. After you score the touchdown, have a good end-zone dance. After you lose, have a good fucking cry. I haven't mastered the cry yet, but I've mastered the middle finger in the air."

That "yet" is pretty telling: Derrick has no plans to stop going for his fourth win. "Thankfully, because of guys like Mark Long and C.T. and Johnny, I feel like I can do this for ten more years. We can do this 'til we're fifty," he says. "I want to continue to have fun with this thing. I want to keep doing cool stuff on the field. I want to keep going into eliminations against fucking big names. I think there's a part of me that I can't escape, a big part of why I think people root for Derrick— he will always somewhat be an underdog, even after three wins. And it's not over! Put your seat belt on."

LANDON LUECK

Champion: *The Inferno II, The Gauntlet 2, Fresh Meat II*

Landon Lueck might just be the quintessential *Challenge* champion. He doesn't hold the record for the most seasons won, or elimination victories, or anything quantifiable like that, but his near-perfect resume and jaw-dropping athletic performances are the stuff of legend. The *Real World: Philadelphia* alum competed in four seasons and won three of them—and the only reason why he didn't win the fourth as well is because of a hotly debated technicality that still haunts him (and fans) all these years later. As a dominant physical beast with a heart of gold, it's not hard to imagine Landon smashing records and becoming the undisputed *Challenge* GOAT, if only he had continued to compete after winning *Fresh Meat II* in 2010. But he never wanted his life to revolve around reality TV, so he made the decision to step away on his own terms to keep his life as normal as possible. It's that responsible and pragmatic way of approaching things that always set him apart from his fellow *Challenge* competitors—and ended up being his secret to success.

When Landon began his reality TV career on *The Real World*, he had to take time off between his junior and senior year of college to make it work. "I was paying my own way in college, and I didn't want to take on any other student loans to try to do this," he says. It was a big decision that he discussed at length with his family, and they came to the conclusion that if he treated his MTV fame like a business—taking advantage of the lucrative appearance and speaking gigs that came after— then taking the risk to pause college would ultimately be worth it. "*The Challenge* wasn't even on my radar. I had just wanted to take part in the entire experience of *The Real World*, and I guess I never really thought that they would want me for anything else. I was thinking that this is my one shot to take advantage of traveling, to be able to get out of Wisconsin for a little bit, and then make some money for college after." It wasn't until he finished filming his season of *The Real World* that he learned about *The Challenge*, which intrigued him. "I was like, 'Okay, I'll just cross my fingers and hope that I do get an invitation.'"

That invitation came immediately after shooting wrapped on *The Real World*. Just a few months later, he was on his way to Mexico for *The Inferno II* in 2005. He was no stranger to competition—he'd been athletic all his life, played every sport in the book, and had built up a lot of muscle mass over the years through powerlifting. By the time he made his *Challenge* debut, though, he'd become a semiprofessional mountain biker, and that sport taught him that being bulky is sometimes disadvantageous. "I had spent a number of years trying to reduce my muscle mass to be faster and lighter for mountain biking. So when *The Challenge* came along, I was at my lightest, which was really good," he says. A common misconception about what it takes to be great at *The Challenge* is that the bigger and stronger you are, the better you'll do, but Landon says that a rock climber's body type is actually best. "I was trying to get to that physique, which is difficult. The strength-to-weight ratio for everybody is critical."

Even though he had never watched a season of *The Challenge* prior to his debut, Landon felt prepared when he arrived for *The Inferno II*, and those first few days in the house felt like a dream. "It was awesome because it was Michelle Pfeiffer's summer home that we were renting, and it had its own private beach that was just incredible," he says. "It was beautiful, and so much better than the house that I had in Philadelphia for *The Real World*. So for me, I thought this is the pinnacle. It was blowing my mind. It was all fun and games. Until it wasn't."

When the real competition began after a few days of partying, Landon finally understood what exactly he had signed up for. "The very first challenge of my very first *Challenge* was the hardest I've ever done," he says. "It was called Surf Torture, and it was a will of attrition. It was just doing simple calisthenics that anyone can do, but for hours. We had these two Navy SEAL guys as drill instructors and if you give up, you had to ring the bell. Of course, you don't want to be the first one out, you don't want to ring the bell, so you literally went until your body gave up. That was my introduction to *The Challenge*."

There was one part of the challenge where Landon had to walk Mike "the Miz" Mizanin like a human wheelbarrow through the ocean, which ended up wearing him down—literally. "I still have scars from that day," he says. "It was brutal. His shoes had sand all over them and the shoes would dig into my arms and after an hour or two, it was just raw." Despite the excruciating pain and exhausting day that seemed like it would never end, giving up wasn't an option for him. "I didn't care if I had to bleed for *The Challenge*, multiple ways, I was there to win."

During that first challenge, Landon noticed that most of his competition didn't share that same passionate drive to win. "I mean, seeing the first half of people drop out so fast, you're like, 'Really? We're just starting,'" he remembers thinking. He learned quickly that a lot of people come on *The Challenge* "just to party and collect their check for the first week." But it was the final few people who kept going for hours whom he needed to watch out for. "You only have a handful of guys and gals that are going to be competition, but those few are *serious* competition."

Landon was never worried about his competition when it came to the physical aspect of the game, however, because the daily challenges were all so unpredictable that he knew he just needed to trust in his abilities. "The political part was always my biggest concern because I'm not a strong politician," he says. "I had to focus on the people who are politicking, because those were the things that could sneak up on you. The physical challenges were very clearly defined, and I'm used to that in my life, but it was the politicking happening after hours that I had to really worry about."

He didn't know he also needed to watch out for people on his own Good Guys team trying to take him out too, but that's exactly what happened. "There was a challenge where you had to pick up these live crabs and you had to transport them, and Darrell [Taylor], who was on my team, completely screwed me over to try to get rid of me. I was blindsided," he says. "He wanted to take home more money, and if he got rid of me, he'd have a bigger piece of the pie. It was a raw introduction to that part of *The Challenge*, where this guy's being nice to you, but he's not really nice. That was specifically when I had the realization that you always have to be watching out for everyone, even people on your team, who are all against you. Keep your friends close but your enemies closer."

It was a hard pill to swallow for Landon, since he really lived up to the Good Guys team name by putting himself into elimination twice, even when he was safe, all to help his team. "I had expected to win, but you never know what could happen," he says of his first two elimination victories. Everything he did worked out in the end because the Good Guys team—Landon, Darrell, Mike, and Jamie Chung—defeated the Bad Asses in the final and won *The Inferno II*, making him a champion in his rookie season. "I never doubted myself, and I never doubted my team." While Darrell had previously tried to sabotage Landon, they were now in the final together, so there was no longer any benefit to screwing over your own teammate. "I was very confident that, unless something really weird happened or somebody was sandbagging because they had some agreement with the other team, we were going to win. It was just one of those days that you had to put one foot in front of the other and just get it done and we would win."

During the final, the Bad Asses teammates kept yelling at each other, and Landon thinks the key to the Good Guys winning was how they stayed positive and supported each other the entire way. "That's one of the things that is the common thread through all my *Challenge* victories—being positive with your teammates is the best thing you can do," he says. "If you're going to just rip your teammate apart like I've seen done time and time again, it doesn't help. And if you think you're going to be on other *Challenge*s, people are going to really dislike you for that."

Throwback Landon, not too far off from current Landon.

Seeing how positive encouragement led his team to victory solidified Landon's number one strategy moving forward: "It's always the right move to be positive and optimistic with your teammate, even if it doesn't look good," he says. "And sometimes it did look bleak, but at the end of the day, you have to remember you've got this opportunity to do all these fun things no one else gets to do, so try to have as much fun as possible."

When Landon returned for *The Gauntlet 2* the next season on the Rookies team, he knew he had to keep a better eye on the politics of the house, but he didn't want to get tangled up in that drama, either. "This time, I was much more aware that people would try to win it any way they can," he says. "Some people like Evan [Starkman], Johnny [Devenanzio], and Kenny [Santucci] played both sides of that really hard. I always tried to avoid those guys because I can't stomach it. I wanted to meet people because they're genuinely interesting, fun, and great souls."

Landon made it to the end of *The Gauntlet 2* without having to compete in a single elimination, and he was once again confident that his team was going to win the final, which they did. "It was clear that we were going to win, so our morale was pretty high throughout the whole thing," he says. "The one brutal part was we did this moving human pyramid, and I was on the bottom. We had knee pads, but we had to move for like a hundred yards, so the skin on all of our knees had come off. And that was halfway through, so you still have to compete the rest of the time with no skin on your knees. There was a lot of blood, we were on the beach so there was sand getting in, and it just wasn't pleasant, to say the least."

Now an undefeated two-time champion, Landon had a seemingly bright future ahead of him on *The Challenge*. But he didn't return until six seasons later for *The Duel II* in 2009. "They didn't call me," he says. "I was just going to let it be. I wasn't going to beg to be on, that's not my style. It was three years and then I finally got the call, and when I found out it was New Zealand, I was ecstatic." That was the main selling point for Landon: getting an all-expenses-paid trip to New Zealand filled with once-in-a-lifetime adventures. "I've always looked at this whole thing as a one-shot deal. There's no contract. There's no guarantee. Take advantage of what it is when it's there. I showed up to that *Challenge* with a tent, a sleeping bag, and a full backpack, because in my mind, I was staying until the end and then taking two weeks to travel in New Zealand."

A lot had changed in the six seasons that Landon was away, however. The rules were now stricter. They were filmed twenty-four hours a day, seven days a week, with no time away from the cameras (the cast used to have a few days off every week when the film crew left them alone). There was no way to escape the game anymore. "We were now on lockdown," he says. "It became a social experiment. It was very stressful. I understand why they wanted to create that pressure cooker for TV, but it was a lot less fun as a cast member. I mean, we had twelve large, grown men sleeping in one bedroom on bunk beds." He wasn't surprised when things got chaotic and violent as early as they did (when C.T. Tamburello and Adam King's fight got them both kicked off before the first challenge even began). "I'd signed up for it; however, it took away a lot of what was so enjoyable about *The Challenge* to me."

He tried to stay out of the drama as much as possible by reading books he'd brought with him as a mental escape. "I was the one who got books taken off the list of things you could bring to a *Challenge*, because I read four books during that *Challenge*," he says with a laugh. "I just kept to myself because I was there to win. I was doing what I needed to do to keep my head clear for the next day."

That strategy clearly worked for him because he dominated most of that season, winning half of the daily challenges and an elimination against Isaac Stout. But when he was sent into the last elimination of the season against Brad Fiorenza, Landon's undefeated streak was finally broken—and the circumstances surrounding his loss made it even more tragic. Brad was given the first point on a murky technicality, and then just barely beat Landon in the third round for the tiebreaker. For the first time in his *Challenge* career, Landon lost. "That was so brutal," he says. "I was winning everything throughout the season, and [executive producer] Justin Booth even took me aside and was like, 'We should call this *The Landon Challenge*, this is crazy.' I was having so much fun, so it was easy to compete. I just wasn't ready for how intense Brad was going to be."

The elimination was a physical battle where the men had to rip a giant carabiner clip off their opponent's back and hook it on the hoop dangling above them. As Landon remembers it, he had to wrestle Brad to get to the clip, and yet host T.J. Lavin yelled at Landon for doing just that, which was confusing. "The rules were so wishy-washy," he says. "In my mind, this was wrestling, and Brad wasn't a wrestler, so I was overconfident. Even after I got penalized, I still felt like there was no chance I was going to lose."

Landon's shoulder got dislocated in the third round, and he *still* almost beat Brad. But Brad's quick thinking to knock Landon's hoop out of the way bought him the time he needed to squeeze out the win in the final second. "I was just shattered. It was crushing," Landon says. "It still haunts me. I went to the hospital after and later had surgery on my shoulder, but I don't think it would've come into play if I had stayed for the final. I would've won." Landon laughs as he apologizes for getting "super cocky," but he believes if that elimination turned out differently, *The Duel II* would have been his third *Challenge* championship. "I feel very strongly after watching the final, because most of it was mountain biking, I was like, 'Oh my god, you've got to be kidding me, this *Challenge* was set up for me,'" he says. "It definitely was more salt in the wound, but I rationalize it as if I would've won that, MTV never would've called me back for anything again. And in my mind, that means I never would've been called for *Fresh Meat II*."

Landon took a season off before returning for his fourth and final *Challenge* appearance in 2010—and he saved his best performance for last. "My whole game strategy was just trying to win it straight-up with as little politicking as possible," he says. "But I knew it was going to be an uphill battle." He had been drafted eighth to pick his *Fresh Meat* partner, which is how he ended up with his last choice, Carley Johnson, who had some of the worst stats across the board. "I was like, 'Yeah, I'm totally screwed.'" He expected their team to come in last every time, but he vowed to never take his frustrations out on his partner. And he soon started to realize that while Carley wasn't the strongest competitor, she had heart—and that was more important than anything else. "She gave it one hundred percent every time. Even the best people sometimes don't give it their all. But she was pretty hardheaded from the beginning, even when things got really scary."

To everyone's surprise, Landon and Carley ended up winning two daily challenges that season. But their biggest and most shocking victory came during their second Exile elimination. They had won their first—a race up a mountain carrying 100 pounds and solving different puzzle checkpoints along the way—and Landon was impressed with Carley's puzzle skills, but nothing could prepare them for the second. This time, the race up the steep mountain was overnight and the weight they had to carry increased to 150 pounds. To this day, it remains one of the toughest eliminations *The Challenge* has ever seen. Landon and Carley faced off against Evelyn Smith and Luke Wolfe, who crossed the finish line first but skipped the last puzzle, giving Landon and Carley the chance to win if they finished it within five minutes. Carley became so delirious that she barely crossed the finish line, but with Landon's constant encouragement they were able to pull off the upset and win with a few minutes to spare. "When I saw it on TV, I was pretty amazed myself," Landon says. "The amount of weight, how far we went, and it being at nighttime, it was so disorienting. Evelyn and Luke made a bad calculated decision. I mean, they shouldn't have lost that—my partner was completely out of it. She was losing it. I was carrying all the weight, and I was like, 'You just have to get your ass up the mountain. If you can do that, we can win this.' I was shocked and very proud because that was nuts."

Carley completed that last Exile, but the fact that she almost passed out had Landon worried that she couldn't survive the final. When it comes to *The Challenge* finals, you're only as strong as your weakest link, and Carley was undeniably the weakest competitor left in the game. "It was scary because it's like, why are you going into a coma? I don't even understand," he remembers. "It was unnerving to know that my partner could fail when it came down to it. Going into the final, I was terrified about what am I going to be left to do all on my own. I always have an undying optimism to win, but deep in my belly, I knew it just wasn't realistic. Kenny and Laurel [Stucky] were so strong and with what we had in front of us, I had discounted us, to be honest."

Everyone assumed Kenny and Laurel were going to walk away from that final with an easy first-place win—but they all, including Landon, underestimated just how awesome Landon is. He single-handedly dominated the entire final, keeping a solid first-place lead from start to finish, dragging Carley behind him the whole way while carrying a heavy bag on his shoulders. At the very end, he literally pushed her up the snowy mountain (which was so steep it required ice picks) with his head in between her butt cheeks. It was, hands down, one of the most impressive *Challenge* performances of all time. "We started gaining altitude, and then you could look back and see where you were, and we just couldn't see anybody," Landon remembers. "We just kept getting a little further up, a little further up, and then finally we were halfway up and saw Kenny and Laurel starting at the bottom. That's when I was like, 'There's no freaking way they're catching us. You can't make up that much time, even with my head up some chick's ass.' From that point on, it was steady as she goes, just get this chick up to the top."

Even with the finish line in sight, Landon knew Carley was running on fumes of fumes, and he couldn't risk her quitting so close to winning. "I was just trying to be as motivating as possible, just to get her body to keep going forward," he says. "Sometimes you push someone too far and they're like, 'Screw you, I'm sitting right here.'" His strategy of keeping calm, positive, and patient-yet-firm with Carley was exactly what she needed. Even when she fell down, totally exhausted, she would immediately get back up and never once considered quitting on Landon. "And there was no rush. Once we got up to the top, we had to wait, like, forty minutes for them anyway."

More than ten years later, fans still call Landon a superhero for what he pulled off in that final, but Landon gets surprisingly humble while talking about it. "It's flattering," he says. "It's hard to compare because every *Challenge* is different. Anytime somebody wins, they've done the right combination of things to be crowned a champ and so they deserve it." It's no contest for Landon, though—*Fresh Meat II* was the most difficult of all his wins . . . which is why it was the most satisfying as well. "It was the first time I felt like an underdog. I'll never forget it. I still have that ice pick in my closet somewhere."

He's also proud that, against all odds, he succeeded while still being able to stick to his philosophy of supporting his partner through positive reinforcement and staying optimistic. The experience impacted him on a deep level, which is why he continues to put that into practice every day in his marriage. "Seeing the success that I had on the shows, where I was strapped in with a female partner and the way that my positivity was received, that reminds me to be a kinder husband and to be motivating and to be a supportive teammate with my wife," he says. "It's kind of weird how it was good for my personal life, because it really taught me to be that person off camera with my loved ones. The love you put in is the love you get out."

Winning *Fresh Meat II* in such a definitive way made it an easy decision for Landon to walk away from *The Challenge*. "I'm done here," he remembers thinking at the time. "It was a nice cap to my twenties and felt like a turning of the page for me, personally. If I didn't win . . . I don't know, maybe I would've kept going back until I won again, so it's probably a good thing I won so I could get back to my real life and my career." He's not tempted to return to the cutthroat world of *The Challenge* anymore, and he gets all the competition he needs at work these days. "I help design dental offices, and I'm one of the top guys in our company when it comes to sales and all that. I do enjoy that competition and it helps drive me toward my goals. *The Challenge* taught me how to be competitive but not an asshole, and that helps me every day. But also, nothing is as stressful as *The Challenge*, so in normal life, you can just relax and don't need to worry about throat-slitting."

But just because Landon isn't interested in coming back to *The Challenge* now, that doesn't mean he hasn't thought about it over the years. He admits that he's considered returning more than once, first for the *Champs vs. Pros* spin-off and more recently for *All Stars*. He was actually invited to compete on *All Stars* but ultimately said no because he can't take that much time off work. "Me and my wife have the life that we've always dreamed of," he says. "Going back into a highly visible role like that changes everything that we have. She's never seen an episode of me on anything, so she's highly anxious of how that would change our life. Feeling normal is important to me, and important to us. MTV was a very, very exciting, cool chapter of my life, but there's more chapters to be written."

But there's still hope, as Landon adds, "I'll never say never."

THE FOUR-TIME CHAMP

DARRELL TAYLOR

Champion: *The Gauntlet, The Inferno, The Inferno II, Fresh Meat* (plus *Champs vs. Pros*)

Darrell Taylor has done something no one else ever has on *The Challenge*. The *Road Rules: Campus Crawl* alum won four seasons in a row, beginning with his rookie season, *The Gauntlet* in 2004, and ending with his fourth season, *Fresh Meat* in 2006. His winning streak was on track to continue with his fifth season, *The Ruins* in 2009, until a night of drinking resulted in a physical fight with his own ally Brad Fiorenza that got Darrell sent home immediately, forever altering the course of *The Challenge* history, both in the rules of how competitors were allowed to drink on the show and halting Darrell's winning trajectory. (To say that night was infamous would be a massive understatement.) But even without that fifth consecutive win, still to this day, no one has ever come close to breaking Darrell's impressive record.

While he hasn't been able to get his long-awaited fifth win, despite five attempts on the main franchise and close calls on three seasons of *All Stars*, Darrell's legacy will always be cemented as one of the best players of all time. Just ask any other player or fan who their "Mount Rushmore" top contestants are, and Darrell's name is always included thanks to his resume, his dominating physical skills, and overall intimidating presence. The only thing that's ever scared him is heights, which he blames on his mother, who made him go on a roller coaster when he was five years old, traumatizing him for life. No one ever wants to go against Darrell, but the lofty goal of beating him is now what drives many younger, newer players who want to make a name for themselves by slaying the giant. He is, undeniably, one of the best to ever play the game.

Darrell's background as a champion Golden Gloves boxer and physical trainer gave him the perfect base of physical skills to succeed on *The Challenge*. But if you ask him what his secret to success is, his answer has surprisingly nothing to do with his athletic performance: "The best way to win a *Challenge* is

No one can catch Darrell's record of four consecutive championships.

more political than physical," he says. "And I just get along with people." When he was younger, he bounced around from school to school, constantly having to make new friends, and it turned him into a chameleon who learned how to bond with anyone, anywhere, no matter how different from him they may be. When he arrived on *The Challenge*, he found that served him well, but he went one step further by also unabashedly flirting his way into the hearts of all the women in the *Gauntlet* cast. "Back then, I was more of a ladies' man," he says. "I was a big flirt, and the girls, man—the girls always took care of me." Darrell understood that the women's votes were just as important as—if not more important than—the men's, so he made strong alliances with Rachel Robinson and Veronica Portillo, two of the most dominant female presences on *The Challenge*. "Most of my wins, I have to say, them having my back helped me a lot. They always protected me, and people didn't really even know that. It was like a secret. We just had an understanding that we would never vote for each other."

That's partly why Darrell holds another impressive record that would make any other player jealous: he avoided eliminations for the longest streak in *Challenge* history. He didn't even see the elimination ring until his fourth season on *Fresh Meat*, when he and his partner, Aviv Bruno (formerly Melmed), beat Derrick Kosinski and Diem Brown in the last Exile challenge before the final. "I wasn't worried about eliminations at all back then, thanks to my relationships and because they were scared of me so they didn't want to piss me off," he says.

But there was another reason why no one wanted Darrell to leave the game. "I was there to compete, but I was also there to have fun, so they wanted to keep me around," he says. "Back then, I was the life of the party." Darrell admits that while the cast would never get away with this now, and he isn't sure how he got away with it without production catching him back then, he would sneak liquor in water bottles into challenges and eliminations. He also snuck alcohol into clubs and bars on their nights out that he would share with his castmates so they wouldn't have to spend as much money. "It's the little shit they don't show, like when people wanted to find weed or anything, I'd be the guy to find everything. I was like the go-to man finding mushrooms, anything—even though I didn't do them. So everyone would be like, 'Darrell is cool, don't send him home.'"

While he never intended for that to be part of his winning strategy, he couldn't deny that it worked out better than he expected in his first season. "I just knew I was going to win," he says. "I didn't care what I had to do; it didn't matter. I was young, hungry, in shape, boxing, running every day." And just as he expected, getting to the end of his first season was a breeze. But when he made it to the final, it was the first time he faced a real obstacle when he had to make sure all his *Road Rules* teammates crossed the finish line before the *Real World* team did. "It was hard because we had to carry some of the girls—they were kind of dying—and I'd have to try to keep them motivated to keep going," he says. He pulled from his many years as a personal trainer to figure out how to push them to work harder without going too far. "I tried different things to get people going, distract them or start talking about stuff and keep them moving. Especially back then, I'd see other people be rude, cussing at their teammates. I'd be watching it thinking, 'That's crazy. My mama raised me better.'"

His positive reinforcement worked on his teammates, and the *Road Rules* team won *The Gauntlet*. He got the call shortly after to return for *The Inferno*, and he was ready for a much different experience after winning his rookie season. "I just remember I was like, 'I'm going to go there to have fun, because there's no way I could win two in a row,'" Darrell says. "That was unheard of. And the next thing you know, I'm there and I'm like, wait a minute, I'm seeing the way the game is going and shifting. Somehow, I've got a good chance of winning again."

Darrell thought coming in as a champion meant he'd be targeted right away, so his strategy this time around was to play peacemaker in the house and lie as low as possible. He just never imagined it would work to the point where he once again avoided eliminations and made it all the way to the final. "I would play neutral," he says. "I'm a team player, and I always try to stay positive. And I'm not chaotic. When shit doesn't go right, I'm not going to panic—unless I'm in the air. You could always count on me to keep everybody chill." He found the right balance between following other players' leads and stepping in as a coach when necessary. "I'd pull certain people to the side that's loud so they're not yelling at everybody else. I'm like, 'Yell at me. I can take it.' We're not going to win if we're all arguing with each other. I don't step on people's toes, and I tend to pick and choose my battles."

And while he always asked tons of questions before the daily challenges began to make sure he understood exactly what he was supposed to do (and so he wouldn't accidentally DQ his team), he also knew the right time to shut up. "I say less during deliberation," he says. "There's been times where I knew I was on the chopping block, but then people bail me out because they start acting crazy in deliberation and would get sent in instead." That also extended to how he acted when others were going into elimination. "This is what a lot of people don't do: I give them respect, which means if you're going in elimination and I'm not, and we're going out that night, I'm not going to be prancing around the house because I know I'm safe. A lot of people do that, and it rubs people the wrong way."

For Darrell, everything always came down to staying cool, calm, and collected, no matter the situation in the house. "I stay consistent when people's mood swings are fucking crazy when they're on the chopping block or not on the chopping block," he says. "I mean, I get it. It's human nature. But I just try to put myself in other people's shoes. I'm like, what would I not like? And if I'm going in, I like my space. I don't want people coming up to me saying, 'How you feeling? You okay? You feeling ready?' Get out of my face, I hate that. I'm not trying to worry about it right now."

For the second time, Darrell's social game got him to the final without having to fight for his life in an elimination. But despite this season's final being exponentially easier than his first one, he was worried his *Road Rules* team was going to lose to the *Real World* team this time. "The final was short and was, like, all these silly carnival games. We never even left the beach." Since it wasn't a miles-long trek up a mountain, Darrell didn't feel confident until they crossed the finish line, because a lot relied on chance. "That's the closest final I've ever been in. We were neck and neck the whole time and people were messing up and you'd have to restart. It was weird. I was like, 'We're about to fucking lose.'" But thanks to a little bit of luck, they won in the end, and to this day, Darrell is still shocked that his team was somehow able to pull it off.

Now that he was officially a two-time champ, when he returned for his third season, *The Inferno II* in 2005, he thought going for the three-peat was impossible. Sensing a pattern here? "I was like, there's no way in hell I could win *three* in a row, so now let's really have some fun," he says. "And that's when I met Derrick. I had a big bottle of Absolut I had got from the duty-free shop, and I know you're not supposed to open it, but whatever, I opened it anyway. Derrick was the only one who wanted to drink with me, so that whole flight to Manzanillo, Mexico, we were tearing it up on the plane. And ever since then, we've been cool as hell. He's my best friend from the show."

That friendship became one of Darrell's most important *Challenge* alliances, on *The Inferno II*, even though they were on separate teams, and for many future seasons. But despite Darrell having such strong relationships with people on both teams, he still expected to end up in an elimination that season, and he was ready for it even though he didn't want to risk his game. "A lot of people think I'm always trying to weasel my way out, but no, I'm just not going to volunteer to go in. You never know what's going to happen, and I don't have anything to prove. But I'll go in if I have to." And if his team had decided he needed to go into the elimination because he was performing the worst out of everyone, then he wouldn't have argued. But he was saved when the team chose to pull names out of a hat instead, and Brad ended up going in instead of him. "I felt bad when Brad's name got picked, because Brad was doing way better than me. But they didn't want to go off performance, so things just worked out."

By knowing when to stay quiet, Darrell narrowly avoided that elimination and made his third final in a row. And when he looked at his fellow Good Guys teammates—Landon Lueck, Mike "the Miz" Mizanin, and Jamie Chung—against the Bad Asses team of Derrick, C.T. Tamburello, Abram Boise, Rachel Robinson, Tina Bridges (formerly Barta), Veronica Portillo, and Tonya Cooley, he knew he was about to achieve the impossible again, simply due to how much running the final required. "There was no way in hell we're losing," he says. "We had a solid squad. I was worried about Mike, though—he was dying on that hill. But we did it."

At this point, Darrell had winning *The Challenge* down to a science—a social science, that is. He knew his winning streak had to end eventually, though, so he thought his time was definitely up on *Fresh Meat*. "There's no way I could win *four* in a row, right? But once we get there, and they let us know we have to pull names to pick our rookie partners, the Fresh Meat, I got second pick and I said, 'Oh shit, I'm about to win.' I even told T.J., 'Watch me win this shit.'" Darrell picked Aviv as his partner because she had scored well on the puzzle, plus he knew he had a lot of allies on the veteran side of the cast, so he was in a good spot. The vets all banded together to target *Real World: Austin* cast members, like Wes Bergmann and his partner, Casey Cooper, for the majority of the Exiles, which saved Darrell for most of the season. "I tried to help [Wes], but he was just always popping off at the mouth and getting angry," Darrell says. "And it was just part of the initiation when you're new. They just never did it to me because they liked me too much."

It had to happen at some point, though, and Darrell's luck finally ran out when he found himself in the last Exile before the final. And even though his first elimination was a long time coming, he didn't find himself nervous at all because of his prior experiences in the boxing ring. "That helped a lot because there's nothing like the anxiety of when you know you're going in a ring and someone is trying to hurt you, and this ain't nothing compared to that," he says. He was upset that he had to compete against his best friend, Derrick, but he knew that he and Aviv had a better shot at winning, simply because the bags they had to carry throughout the Exile challenge were lighter than Derrick and Diem's (since it was calculated by how much baggage they brought to that season). "Derrick was already kind of defeated before we started, so that gave me hope. It's more mental than anything, and I never let myself call it before it's over."

After leaving Derrick and Diem in the dust during the last Exile, Darrell and Aviv smoked the competition in the final when they were the only team to solve both puzzles during the ten-mile run on the beach. And even though the other two teams—Tina and Kenny Santucci, and Wes and Casey—got an early lead, Darrell knew that keeping a solid pace throughout the entire race was better than speeding off in the beginning. "It's more like a marathon—it's not a sprint because you're running in sand, and you had to carry these heavy bags," he says. "I've got to give it to Aviv, man, she killed it on those puzzles and we smoked them. When we finished, the sun was up, and when Kenny and Tina and Wes and Casey finished, it was dark."

Because of their strong finish and knowing it was just him and his partner rather than a big team, *Fresh Meat* is Darrell's favorite win out of his four championships. And while the money from all four wins helped him support his family through the years, it's the experiences he got from those seasons traveling to Mexico and Australia that gave him a new perspective on how fortunate he really is, not only as a *Challenge* champion but also in his daily life. "I saw a lot of people that don't have it as good as us. I saw a lot of poverty out there, and it made me thankful for everything I have," he says. "I've got all my limbs, I have a roof over my head, I have a car, I can provide for my family. I now know that no matter what little things stress me out, I just know it could always be worse."

And in a full-circle way, that thinking has also helped him cope with the close calls and near misses of his recent *Challenge* seasons. "Those were tough pills to swallow, but I know I got a little big headed," he says. "I got overconfident. I've got to come correct if I ever want to get that next win. And I was so close. It will happen." Since Darrell achieved the impossible season after season at the beginning of his *Challenge* career, he knows that anything is possible now—even getting that elusive fifth win . . . eventually.

THE FIVE-TIME CHAMP

CHRIS "C.T." TAMBURELLO

Champion: *Rivals II, Invasion of the Champions, War of the Worlds 2, Double Agents, Spies, Lies & Allies* (plus *Champs vs. Stars, Champs vs. Stars 2*)

If there's an award for most improved *Challenge* competitor of all time, Chris "C.T." Tamburello wins. There's no debate. The bruiser from Boston exploded onto the show with a "punch first, ask questions later" mentality that earned him the "honor" of being the only contestant to be kicked off *The Challenge* twice for physical violence. He was his own worst enemy—his temper held him back for so long that he holds the record for being the male champion who took the longest to get his first win, clocking in at nine seasons. But when C.T. finally learned from his mistakes, he didn't just improve his strategy—he perfected it.

The *Real World: Paris* alum went on to become one of the best *Challenge* champions of all time by constantly evolving his physical, political, social, and mental game, flawlessly dominating in every aspect of the competition—and he keeps getting better and better at it, delivering some of his best work in his two most recent seasons. He's been in ten finals, more than any other competitor, and he's won the most money: $1.365 million. He's been called "a freak of nature," the "puzzle master," a strategic mastermind with the brains to back up the brawn. To quote his own *Rivals II* partner, Wes Bergmann: "The man legitimately scares me to death."

After more than eighteen years on the franchise, C.T.'s gone from being the young hothead to being the elder statesman, and he's watched new young bucks enter the game and make the same mistakes he did at the beginning of his career. He gives them the same advice he wished he knew back when he debuted on *The Inferno* in 2004: "There's a fine line between arrogance and confidence, and if you're not careful, pride can be your own worst enemy,"[*] he said in an interview with *Entertainment Weekly*. "*The Challenge*, you don't know what to expect, just take it as it comes. If I were to toot my own horn, I would say that's probably my biggest strength, being able to adapt."[†]

He immediately showed how much potential he had as a competitor in his rookie season, winning four Life Shields, throwing himself into an elimination to save a teammate, and achieving the impossible: looking intimidating while eating cookies and drinking milk. He sent Shane Landrum home and made it to the final on the *Real World* team, but eventually lost to the *Road Rules* team. He returned for *The Inferno II*, winning an impressive six Life Shields, avoiding every elimination, and made it to yet another final on the Bad Asses team, losing once again.

---

[*] Sydney Bucksbaum, "*The Challenge: Double Agents* Winners Break Down That Dominating Final Run," EW.com, *Entertainment Weekly*, April 21, 2021.

[†] Sydney Bucksbaum, "CT Tamburello Addresses His Future on *The Challenge*," EW.com, *Entertainment Weekly*, December 16, 2021.

The Duel was a real turning point for C.T. Meeting Diem Brown cracked his tough, bad-boy exterior, and as fans and other cast members watched them fall in love that season, C.T. started to show there was so much more to him than meets the eye. He continued to perform impressively in the game, too. He beat Evan Starkman in an elimination, but a frustrating design flaw in an elimination against Brad Fiorenza sent him home on a technicality. After two seasons where he came so close to winning, watching C.T. leave right before the final was heartbreaking—but the rough times were only just beginning.

C.T. came in hot the next season on *The Inferno 3*, punching Davis Mallory in the face and getting kicked off before the game even began. Perhaps that's why he was more determined to win than ever the next season on *The Gauntlet III*. His performance showed he would stop at nothing to finally cross that finish line in first place and become a champion. The Veterans team slaughtered the Rookies, winning almost every single challenge. But C.T. made a fatal error early in the season that doomed his entire team when he convinced everyone to vote Johnny "Bananas" Devenanzio into an elimination instead of Eric "Big Easy" Banks. He was more focused on getting revenge on Johnny than making a smart play, and it cost him dearly. During the final, Big Easy collapsed and had to be medically disqualified from the game, so even though the Veterans crossed the finish line long before the Rookies, they had to forfeit the win. It was a devastating end to what should have been C.T.'s first win.

Things went from bad to worse when C.T. returned for *The Duel II* in 2009. He was grieving the loss of his brother, Vincent Tamburello Jr., who had recently been murdered, and still coping with his breakup with Diem. Shortly after arriving in New

Zealand, he got into a vicious fight with Adam King that got them both kicked off the show.

After a three-season break, C.T. made his epic return in what instantly became one of the most iconic *Challenge* moments of all time. As Johnny and Tyler Duckworth were preparing to face off with each other in an elimination on *Cutthroat*, C.T. emerged from the shadows as a Mercenary instead, looking leaner, meaner, and more intensely focused on destroying his competition than he'd ever been before. With Johnny strapped to him like a backpack, C.T. stood up, sumo-stomped his way across the floor, and threw Johnny into a barrel—Johnny never stood a chance. Tyler put up more of a fight in the next round, but C.T.'s performance had everyone in shock. It was an incredible return to form that kicked off the next era of C.T.'s *Challenge* career where he buckled down and got serious about winning.

But while he worked on keeping his temper in check, he'd already made enemies—as in, an entire house of them who were all working together with one goal: eliminate C.T. at all costs. On *Rivals*, C.T. was partnered with Adam, and while they actually managed to put their differences aside to perform well in challenges together, they were fighting an uphill battle the entire time, since the majority of the cast banded together as "the mob" working to eliminate their team. Evan even threw a challenge so that he and his partner, Nehemiah Clark, could face C.T. and Adam in an elimination, but that backfired, and C.T. and Adam won. The mob finally got their wish when C.T. and Adam lost to Johnny and Tyler in the last elimination before the final.

If C.T. thought working with Adam was awkward, he had no idea what was in store for him next. On *Battle of the Exes* in 2012, he reunited with Diem when they were forced to partner up. They went from barely speaking at the beginning of the season to coming together as a powerhouse team by the end in one of the most compelling narrative arcs *The Challenge* has ever delivered. And while they won the last two challenges and dominated for the majority of the final, C.T. gassed out in the last leg of the hike up the Icelandic mountain, allowing Johnny and Camila Nakagawa to pass him. C.T. and Diem finished in second place, adding yet another near win to his resume.

By the time C.T. arrived in Thailand for *Rivals II*, he was more than primed to finally win. And with Wes as his partner, he had a solid shot. They made a formidable pair, and they proved they were the team to beat during one challenge in particular: Rampage. C.T. and Wes were the only team to transfer all twenty balls from one end of the half-pipe ramp to the other. Meanwhile, Johnny ended up lying on the ground and puking after only three minutes. It was a spectacular showing that foreshadowed their eventual win in the final, as C.T. and Wes never once gave up their lead over the course of the two-day race.

C.T. didn't just dominate the game physically on *Rivals II*. He also displayed a new—albeit extremely ruthless and, at times, problematic—understanding and skill for the political and social sides of the game, as he flirted with and manipulated the women for their votes all season. He still had some blowups and missteps that proved he didn't have full control over his temper yet, but it all worked out in the end. "I did it. I finally won *The Challenge*," C.T. said. "It took me ten years, but me and Wes, we made it. It is fair to say that me and Wes are no longer rivals."[*]

When C.T. returned immediately the next season for *Free Agents*, he proved that his *Rivals II* win wasn't a fluke. He delivered a powerful individual performance, won a tough elimination

---

[*] *MTV's The Challenge*, episode 12, season 24, September 24, 2013.

against Leroy Garrett, and almost made it to another final. But in a major upset for the puzzle master himself, Johnny beat him in the last elimination of the season, which was a series of puzzles.

C.T.'s next season looked even more promising, as he was partnered with Diem once again for *Battle of the Exes II*. Considering how well they'd worked together last time and how close they'd come to winning, it seemed as if this was their season to lose. However, in a tragic twist of fate, Diem had to exit the game in the third episode when her cancer came back for the third time, and C.T. left with her. She died a few months later, and C.T. was at her hospital bedside before she passed. "Our plan to be together forever hasn't changed, it's just going to take a little longer now. And I'm going to hold onto this ring for you till we are together again," he wrote on Instagram at the time, calling her the love of his life.[*]

After a two-year break, C.T. returned to *The Challenge* for *Invasion of the Champions*, and it was like he was a whole new man. He proudly revealed that, in his time away from the show, he'd become a father, and it changed him on the inside *and* outside. He self-deprecatingly dubbed this new chapter of his *Challenge* career as the "dadbod era" in honor of his new physique, and declared that he was now here to win for his son. "I didn't want to end my career on *The Challenge* the way it ended on the last one before this,"[†] he said. He beat Darrell Taylor in one of the most impressive Knot So Fast eliminations of all time—"Production

[*] Allison Takeda, "Diem Brown's Love Chris 'CT' Tamburello Shares Touching Instagram Tribute: 'You Have Always Been My Angel'" *Us Weekly*, November 19, 2014.

[†] Ale Russian, "*The Challenge: Invasion of the Champions* Winners Speak! Who's Quitting after This Season and Who Might Become the Next Bananas?" EW.com, *Entertainment Weekly*, May 9, 2017.

had to cut that rope off with a chainsaw, it was that tight,"[*] he said—and finally won his second championship.

"I didn't expect to make it that far, never mind win it," he said. "At first, I went on it because I wanted to do it for my son. I knew the time was gonna come when he was gonna be old enough to understand his old man was on TV and I didn't want him to see me as some knucklehead punk running around with his head cut off. I wanted him to see me as I am today. I think I accomplished that. But then over time, it became about me and getting my confidence back and standing on my own feet and showing that I still have it. To me, this one was the most special."[†]

The way C.T. evolved his game during *Invasion* was obvious—becoming a father had simply calmed him down exponentially. "Being a dad changes things," he says. "You definitely think about your actions before you act. It's nice when people say that—that they actually see that change. And when people say I've changed for the better, it means a lot."[‡] He also credits his son for helping him hone a very important skill set necessary to do well on *The Challenge*: "There's nothing like having a five-year-old who you can do puzzles with all the time, I swear to god."[§]

With C.T. now a two-time champ, his next few seasons flew by with a string of losses. On *XXX: Dirty 30*, he delivered one hell of a season, winning almost every challenge, but finished the

---

[*] Sydney Bucksbaum, "CT Teases *The Challenge: Total Madness*: 'It Was Just a MINDF—,'" EW.com, *Entertainment Weekly*, March 31, 2020.

[†] Russian, "*The Challenge: Invasion of the Champions* Winners Speak!"

[‡] Ibid.

[§] Bucksbaum, "CT Tamburello Addresses His Future on *The Challenge*."

final in third place. He was partnered with Veronica Portillo on *Final Reckoning* and barely competed before they were unceremoniously sent home without even getting the chance to fight for their spot in an elimination. On *War of the Worlds*, a rookie called him out in an early elimination to try to make a name for himself by toppling a *Challenge* legend. It backfired for the rookie, and C.T. was collateral damage after losing the three-way elimination to Kyle Christie.

He finally broke his losing streak in *War of the Worlds 2*, although the season started off rocky for him when he entered the game as a Reinforcement (aka team leader) and was rejected by all his fellow vets on Team USA. He was forced to join Team UK, and while they lost most of the challenges, C.T. was able to hone a new political strategy where he stayed neutral and out of the drama as long as possible, and it ended up keeping him out of elimination all season. "There's a difference between staying neutral and being a floater," he said. "If you're a floater, you're everybody's best friend, you try to stay below the radar. Being neutral is you're not everybody's best friend—you're nobody's friend, so to speak . . . I'd like to think I've done these long enough where I do a good job of being patient before making decisions because once you make your decision, it's final. If you pick the wrong alliance, the wrong move, there's no coming back from it."[*]

It worked, and C.T. went on to get his third *Challenge* championship, winning with his teammates, Jordan Wiseley, Rogan O'Connor, and Dee Nguyen. It was clear a new era of C.T.'s career was starting to emerge as he became a top political

---

[*] Sydney Bucksbaum, "*The Challenge: Total Madness* Eliminated Player Admits His Shocking Loss 'Was a Wake-up Call,'" EW.com, *Entertainment Weekly*, April 15, 2020.

player out of necessity. "I've never had the experience of being someone's number one; I've always been the lone wolf down at the bottom of the chain," he said. "I think me being on the outside looking in, it worked to my advantage because I can always pop in every once in a while, say a piece or two, and try to nudge alliances in certain directions, and then act like it wasn't my idea, and then somehow end up in the final. 'I'm still here!'"[*]

The next season, however, introduced a new twist that shook everything up: in order to be eligible to run the final, players must win an elimination. C.T. adapted quickly, wasting no time in sending himself in against rookie/*Survivor* alum Jay Starrett in a challenge similar to Knot So Fast for the chance to secure his Red Skull early, but he lost in a shocking upset. "I thought I was walking away with it," C.T. said. "This is why you never take anything for granted in *The Challenge*. It was carelessness on my part. Maybe I was tired. Let's be honest, I look so out of shape, if you ask me. It looks like I just got off my championship parade. I'm not happy with it, but it was a wake-up call. I mean, I looked like a stuffed pig on camera. I came in still floating on my last win, and I was just too comfortable. I got lazy, and I got caught slipping. I'm going to take this L, I'm going to go back to the drawing board, tighten up, and come back with a chip in my shoulder and some teeth. Statistically, I've done better in the 'dadbod' era. Three of [my wins came] during the 'washed-up' era. Now if I can combine being in shape like I was in the past with the dadbod era where it's about working smarter not harder, I think I have a serious shot."[†]

C.T. came back with a vengeance for *Double Agents*. He used

---

[*] Bucksbaum, "CT Tamburello Addresses His Future on *The Challenge*."

[†] Bucksbaum, "*The Challenge: Total Madness* Eliminated Player Admits His Shocking Loss 'Was a Wake-up Call.'"

C.T.'s history on *The Challenge* is more complicated and tangled than his Knot So Fast performance.

his *Total Madness* loss as serious fuel and returned looking like a whole new guy. The dadbod was gone, replaced with a much more in-shape "fatherly figure," he joked. When the cast was told they were allowed to pick their partner for the season, C.T. rejected Kam Williams in favor of two-time champion Ashley Mitchell, a mistake he paid for immediately when they were targeted for the first elimination. After Ashley was sent home, C.T. was paired up with Tula "Big T" Fazakerley by default. While Big T was one of the weakest athletic competitors in the house, she was a phenomenal social player who ended up teaching C.T. a thing or two about playing like a "born-again rookie" while he coached her on how to win Hall Brawl—although she eventually lost that elimination against *Big Brother* alum Amber Borzotra, who became C.T.'s new partner.

"I really was digging in and learning how to play the game again and establishing new connections and relationships with people and really diving in politically because I lost touch with that because I got too comfortable," C.T. said. "That was a wake-up call for me: Either you adapt to the new game and the way that *The Challenge* is being played now, or you're done. It was sink or swim, and we swam."[*]

C.T. and Amber became a team right before the final began, and although they had never worked together before, they were unstoppable. "It's crazy, we won every single checkpoint," C.T. said. "I think at one point we had a lead of close to an hour. I'm going to be honest, I don't think anyone was catching us. I think it was the best run I've ever had in the final."[†]

After winning one of the most intense seasons yet, C.T. came back immediately for the next one, somehow in even better shape than before and with a new appreciation for how to play the social and political game. He should have had the biggest target on his back as a four-time reigning champ, and yet he quietly manipulated the game on *Spies, Lies & Allies* from the sidelines and kept himself out of every single elimination. And after a dominating physical performance in the final, he won his fifth championship. "This one was important because I felt like it's the cherry on top for me feeling secure in myself again," he said. "I came out of retirement, and to me it was kind of like, I won, but I won my life back. It's been a long road to get to here and there was a long time during the 'dadbod' era where I was kind of in a dark place, I was going through a lot. I kind of basically had to rebuild. For some reason, it was just like if I could win here, I can win back home. To win this one and go back-to-back, to be doing as well as I have been on *The Challenge*, it was like, I'm doing alright again. Finally, I felt like

---

[*] Bucksbaum, "*The Challenge: Double Agent* Winners Break Down That Dominating Final Run."

[†] Ibid.

I'm in control. I'm on top. If I rode off into the sunset, I could ride off with my head high and be like, I did it. There's nothing else for me to prove, not to myself, not to anybody."[*]

Having recently turned forty, C.T. is proud to look back and see how much he's grown up and changed for the better thanks to *The Challenge*. "I don't feel like there's any competition for me. I was always my worst enemy, and I feel like I won—I beat myself at my own game," he said. "Part of me thinks that the game is changing and part of me thinks I'm just getting old. I can't play the same games that I used to. I keep telling myself it's not going to last much longer and then I win. Everyone's like, 'Why don't you just retire?' I don't have it in me to ever say I'm going to retire. What else would I do? I've got some left in the tank, I want to ride it out. Let's see how long it lasts!"[†]

Right now, however, he wants to focus on spending time with his family, as well as building up his acting career. He shot his first major lead movie role in the *Most Dangerous Game* remake in 2021, fulfilling a lifelong dream of his, but he promises his first love will always be *The Challenge*. "I got lucky when I went to a *Real World* casting I found on flyers they were passing out at a club I was bartending at in college. And I didn't know those fifteen minutes would last fifteen years," he said. "Every year since then, I get whisked off to this magical land, I've gone to every country, every continent except for the South Pole, doing crazy obstacles, jumping out planes, bungee jumping. Why do I keep coming back? Why *not* come back?!"[‡]

---

[*] Bucksbaum, "CT Tamburello Addresses His Future on *The Challenge*."

[†] Ibid.

[‡] Bucksbaum, "CT Teases *The Challenge: Total Madness*."

THE SEVEN-TIME CHAMP

JOHNNY "BANANAS" DEVENANZIO

Champion: *The Island*, *The Ruins*, *Rivals*, *Battle of the Exes*, *Free Agents*, *Rivals III*, *Total Madness* (plus *Champs vs. Stars*)

No one knows more about winning *The Challenge* than Johnny "Bananas" Devenanzio. He's won seven seasons, making him the most decorated *Challenge* champion of all time. But he's also experienced the extreme opposite end of that spectrum—he's been the first one eliminated from a season, and he's lost more eliminations than he's won. From the highs to the lows, he's been through it all—which makes sense, given that he also holds the record for the most seasons competed in by a single player. Johnny might just have the most unique and thorough understanding of every single facet of this game, better than any other player who's ever appeared on *The Challenge*. And throughout all his experiences, from his most impressive triumphs to his downright embarrassing blunders, he's realized that succeeding in this game boils down to one relatively simple idea.

"As Darwin says, in nature, it's not the strongest nor the smartest that survive—it's the ones who have the ability to adapt," Johnny says. "*The Challenge* is a constantly evolving, changing landscape, whether it's the people, the format of the game, how there's a twist around every corner. So it's the people who are able to adapt and pivot and adjust to this ever-changing landscape who do the best. That's where I attribute most of my success to: my ability to adapt." Even with his legendary record, he'll be the first to admit he's not the biggest, strongest, or smartest player in any season he's competed on, but he's never let that hold him back. "I'm like a chameleon, and that's what's helped me, not in just the show, but in life as well." It took a lot of trial and error for Johnny to figure out his winning strategy, and his refusal to give up after each mistake and to instead dedicate himself to learning to grow from each one became one of his best qualities as a competitor.

The *Real World: Key West* alum had one of the worst debuts ever on *The Challenge*—he literally could not have done worse if he tried. "I remember getting the call and being super excited about the prospect of going on *The Duel*," he says. "And then I was the first one eliminated. This was my opportunity to make a name for myself and make my mark on *The Challenge*, and I'm the first one gone. It ended as quickly as it started." As a rookie, Johnny knew from the start it was highly unlikely he'd win that season. He actually cared more about proving himself as a worthy competitor and creating a legacy worth remembering, which made his eventual physical, social, and political failures even more devastating. "I was fresh off my *Real World* season, and I was just in full-on party mode," he says. "Going on *The Challenge*, I went in with the same mentality. What I didn't realize is the game had already begun before I knew it." Like many other competitors in their first season, he was oblivious to the politicking and strategizing going on behind the scenes.

Despite having a solid foursome alliance with his *Real World* castmates—Tyler Duckworth, Paula Beckert (formerly Meronek), and Svetlana Shusterman—Johnny got played immediately. "Everyone else was plotting against us because we were the new kids, and we got picked off," he says. "I immediately realized after that season if you're not playing the game, the game is playing you. It's like being at a poker table: if you can't spot the sucker, then you are the sucker." He lost to his own ally Tyler in a watermelon-lifting contest. As Johnny was leaving, host T.J. Lavin gave him advice that's always stuck with him. "I called out Tyler at thirty-one watermelons, and I ended up putting my stake in the game in his hands. T.J. told me after, 'You never want to put your fate in someone else's hands.' That rang true."

It's safe to say Johnny's first season was a disaster, and his story could have easily ended there. But instead of accepting his rookie debut as a total failure, he chose to use it as a tool instead. "I almost think that me being eliminated first made me respect the game even more," he says. "That early dismissal is what really fueled my fire to be better. We only used to do a *Challenge* once a year, so I had quite a bit of time to sit around and think and figure out what my next move was. My whole goal was to go into the next season and not repeat the same mistakes."

When he returned the next season for *The Inferno 3*, he course-corrected immediately. He went from being the first one eliminated to making it all the way to the final without seeing a single elimination. His Good Guys team lost in the final—"We got our asses beat pretty bad," he admits—but he still considers that season to be a win, because he proved he could change and adapt as a player by fixing his previous mistakes. "I went in with my head down and shut up and listened, and just was a team player," he says. "I went into *The Duel* as a rookie but had acted as if I was one of the top guys there. I came in way too hot. I just rubbed a lot of people the wrong way—which is kind of what I've done over my entire career, but now I knew I needed to work to manage that."

During *The Inferno 3*, Johnny also started to realize that, despite not being the biggest or most feared guy on the cast, there was still a way he could excel in the physical parts of the game. "I need to make people see me as a dominant or intimidating physical competitor through my performance in the challenges," he says. "The only way to do that is to show them. I can't convince or tell them. I just needed to put my head down and go to work and show that I'm worthy to be here. I noticed the majority of challenges we do involve agility and endurance, not strength, so that's what I started focusing on." By training to be a more well-rounded athlete, he knew he'd be better prepared for whatever unpredictable situation he'd get thrown into. He had a solid athletic background—growing up, he played a lot of different sports like soccer, baseball, tennis, and roller hockey—but he found that activities like surfing, skateboarding, and snowboarding helped build up his body control, something he's noticed a lot of competitors lack. "If you want to gauge a guy's athleticism, you watch how they throw and catch a ball," he says. "We'll show up on day one of a *Challenge*, and we'll toss a ball around, and some guys who are built like professional athletes look like a newborn baby deer trying to catch a ball. And it's those skills that translate into the game." And as he had learned his first season, the game is always happening, even when other players don't realize it, so now Johnny paid attention to every detail, no matter how small. "I'm always observing people in the house when they're working out or just doing normal things to assess where people's strengths and weaknesses are."

The last piece of Johnny's strategy is based on another one of his mantras: work smarter, not harder. "I am notorious for finding loopholes and punching holes in the game, doing things that aren't necessarily part of the rules but we weren't told we *couldn't* do," he says. "I always try and look for a flaw in the matrix. I think that just comes from how I've lived my life—I've always wanted to find the easiest way to do things. I've always been a critical thinker, and I've always been good at figuring out how to build things or how things go together, so I started applying that to *The Challenge*."

Johnny tested out that strategy during the first challenge on *The Gauntlet III*, and it worked better than he could have predicted. "We had to run through this mud pit to retrieve balls that were on the other side, and you could line up wherever you wanted," Johnny remembers. "Obviously the mud is going to be deeper in the middle, so I lined up all the way to the very far edge, and when T.J. blew the horn, instead of jumping straight to the mud, I'd take five or ten steps on the edge of the pit, which was still solid ground, before getting in the mud. By that point I'd already gained ten steps, and that little idea gave me the edge over everyone else. People told me after, 'You were cheating,' but hey, nobody said anything about it. It's better to ask for forgiveness than for permission." That's why you'll never see him asking T.J. any questions about the rules of each challenge before it starts. "They're not going to disqualify me.

Bananas is the king of finding loopholes to wash away the competition.

They might yell at me, but by that time I might have already done something that put me in the lead, so it's worth the risk."

Love it or hate it, that strategy works: Johnny currently holds the record for the most daily challenge wins of all time. He consistently finds whatever small detail or shortcut gives him any kind of a leg up on the competition, like on *Battle of the Bloodlines* in 2015, when he used his head to smash the crickets and cockroaches he was supposed to catch with his mouth. "It's really difficult to catch a live grasshopper with your mouth," he says. "But if they're dead, they're not trying to get away. The producers were like, 'What the hell is this guy doing?' but it made it so much easier." His latest season, *Total Madness* in 2020, featured his most impressive loophole yet when he outsmarted the entire setup of a daily challenge. "We had to run into this big pit of foam to see this blinking set of lights. You had to memorize them, go back through the foam, and stack colored plates in the correct order of the lights. I noticed before my turn there was this metal box off to the side that was somewhat reflective, and if you stood at the right angle, you could see the reflection of the lights blinking without even going into the foam pit at all. When it was my turn, I didn't even run into the foam and stacked all the disks right away."

As Johnny started to hack challenges successfully first on *The Gauntlet III*, he thought he finally had cracked the code. He was proving himself to be a worthy team player for the Veterans, and they kept winning. "I felt I was in a pretty good position," he says. "But the politicking is what got me. This was back when me and C.T. [Tamburello] still had quite a bit of beef, and I was pretty close to the bottom rung as far as the alliance on our team went, and that ended up biting me in the ass." The first time the Veterans lost a daily challenge, Johnny was thrown into an elimination against Evan Starkman. "That was so annoying. It was a slider puzzle, and my team had just nominated me to go in so they obviously wanted me to go home. My team helped Evan win the puzzle, literally telling him exactly where to slide his pieces, and I'm sitting here trying to do it by myself. I ended up getting the last laugh on that one, though, because instead of getting rid of the biggest, slowest guy, Big Easy [Eric Banks], they sent me in, and keeping Eric around ended up costing them all the final. C.T., to this day, still is like, 'That's the biggest mistake I've ever made on *The Challenge*, making a decision based on my emotions instead of what would've been best for the team.'"

At this point, Johnny was starting to doubt if he'd ever be able to win *The Challenge*, but he kept rolling with the punches. *The Gauntlet III* reminded him how important the political side of the game is, but this time, he realized his mistake was how his rivals got to him before he could get to them, all because they knew he'd eventually try to come for them. "All I had was a hammer, and I looked at everybody as nails," he says. "If I could go back to those early seasons, I'd be like, 'Dude, just be cool. Even if you don't like someone, don't let them know that. Don't go in day one and draw a line in the sand, letting everyone know where they stand with you.' If you could trick your enemies into thinking you're good with them, it's so much easier. Had I not been such a stubborn asshole, maybe things would've worked out differently. But then again, maybe taking that tougher road is what made me even better in the end."

By the time he returned for *The Island* in 2008, Johnny focused on securing his alliance so he didn't get screwed by the politics again. His social game was perhaps the worst it's ever been—he *really* earned his reputation as a *Challenge* villain that season—but, hey, baby steps. "My first three seasons, I had been at the bottom of the pecking order in every alliance I was in, and I had to figure out how to change that," he says. "I ended up being the dominant force in the house that season, and they still tried to get rid of me. Abe [Boise] is basically telling everyone, 'Please send me home, I have business to attend to,' and they *still* tried to send me home. But the numbers I had that season really boded well for me."

His alliance saved him multiple times, and eventually he ended up on a team with Derrick Kosinski, Kenny Santucci, and Evelyn Smith for the final in which they had to race to build a boat and sail it to the finish line. They crushed the other team of Paula, Robin Hibbard, Ryan Kehoe, and Jenn Grijalva, and Johnny finally became a *Challenge* champion. "I just felt like the pressure was all on us, because me, Derrick, Kenny, and Evelyn, that's a pretty solid team," he says. "There's some people who've done fifteen challenges and never won, so for me to be able to win on my fourth one, I felt like I could now be in the conversation as someone who's respected on the show."

His first win immediately led to his second, as he was now qualified to compete on the Champions team on *The Ruins* in 2009. The Champions dominated that entire season, winning every single daily challenge except for one. And while Johnny was once again in the alliance controlling the politics of his team, he was still on the very bottom. "Out of me, Kenny, Evan, and Derrick, I was the only one who had to go into elimination that season, and I realized my role is going to be the guy who's going to get his hands dirty every season. There are certain players that literally every season can go in and never see an elimination, and that will never be me. After that season, I realized that even if we have the numbers, even if we're in control, I'm still going to be the one that's going to have to put in work. I'll never be able to skate to the end." Once he accepted that, he just used it as more motivation. "Ninety percent of the game is mental, and the more you get in your head, the worse you're going to do. Knowing that every season I'm going to have to fight my way through an elimination is beneficial to me. Every season I've won, I had to win an elimination first, and I know I've earned it."

Of course, he'd still rather stay out of eliminations if he can help it. He's learned more than anyone else how unpredictable and uncontrollable eliminations can be. After winning *The Ruins*, he felt like he was at the top of his game when he arrived on *Cutthroat* in 2010. Near the end of the season, he was prepared for an elimination rematch against Tyler. He even volunteered himself to go in, hoping for the chance to redeem his very first loss on *The Duel*. But producers flew in C.T. as a surprise opponent instead in one of the biggest twists in *Challenge* history, and C.T. ended up wearing Johnny like his very own custom Bananas Backpack.

Johnny can laugh about it now, but he admits it was "embarrassing and emasculating" losing so spectacularly in what has become one of the most iconic eliminations of all time. "I realized after that why they have weight classes in boxing and wrestling," he says. "There's literally nothing I could have done any differently to change that outcome. But mostly I realized that *The Challenge* is just like life, in that sometimes, it just ain't fair. And complaining about it won't change a thing. If anything, it just made me want to come back and be that much hungrier to do better, because I've learned I'm more motivated by my failures than I am by my successes—and there's no bigger failure ever than that one."

The Bananas Backpack wasn't the toughest defeat that Johnny's had in his career, however. "There's other losses that I took way harder than that, because I had losses that I could've and should've won had it not been for some bonehead miscalculation or misstep," he says. Losing to Cara Maria Sorbello and Jamie Banks on *Bloodlines* in a puzzle elimination, in an endurance battle against Derrick on *XXX: Dirty 30*, and to Theo Campbell on *War of the Worlds* because he mixed up two Roman numerals all haunt him more than getting carried on C.T.'s back and tossed into a barrel. "Out of all my eliminations, that was just the most one-sided, obviously. It sucked to have to watch that happen on national TV."

As with every previous defeat, Johnny came back more determined than ever to win. That very next season, he was paired up with Tyler on *Rivals*, and they both got their chance at redemption. They won multiple daily challenges, beat C.T. and his partner, Adam King, in an intense Hall Brawl elimination right before the end of the season, and went on to win the first two-day final in *Challenge* history. "That was hands down the most gratifying win, because the way we got there, the road that Tyler and I had to trek to get there, was directly through C.T. in a frigging trench dug in the ground," he says. "To this day, that was the most terrifying elimination I've ever done. *Rivals* was hands down the most difficult final, one of the most difficult *Challenge*s, against the toughest competition, ever. I think the final was twentysomething miles straight, nonstop."

At multiple points during the first day of the final, Johnny doubted that he'd be able to finish. "That was the first time that I really experienced what it felt like to hit your physical and mental wall," he says. "But then you find that there are walls beyond that wall. It was the first time that I pushed my mind and my body to that point and realized I'm capable of more than I thought. It all comes down to heart." Not only surviving but also winning the *Rivals* final changed everything for Johnny moving forward. "I came home having a different outlook on life. Things that I used to find difficult, now I know what real physical pain and difficulty is. I felt like I was a mentally and physically stronger person as a result of it."

That's why he returned the next season for *Battle of the Exes* ready to win again. "Out of all the seasons, I think *Exes* is the one I went into with the most confidence in my abilities," he says. Being forced to work with his ex Camila Nakagawa, however, was a challenge on its own. "I need a partner who is going to listen and who isn't going to argue, and we would argue over everything." He constantly got frustrated with Camila, but admits he isn't the easiest person to work with, either, and their team dynamic was often volatile as a result. "My instinct is to yell at my partner, and sometimes that has the exact desired opposite effect. Some people need to be coddled and patted on the back. Other people need to be yelled at. You've got to figure out what your partner needs, and it all goes back to adapting—you adapt to who you're partnered up with."

Johnny jokes that he went into *The Challenge* with a high school diploma in knowing how to read people, and he left with a master's degree. "*The Challenge* is one big sociology experiment, and it is about understanding people and how they operate in group settings, and you're learning in a group of the most difficult, controversial, insane, unhinged human beings ever," he says. "If you can figure out how to navigate that environment? Dude, real life is *easy*." He's recently realized that *The Challenge* turned out to be the best training for his current job hosting a travel show. "You could literally put me in any environment with any person and I'll thrive. One episode I need to wrestle a six-hundred-pound sumo man, the next I'm in the south of France drinking wine with the biggest wine producer in the country, the next show I'm in Provincetown, Massachusetts, talking about art, and I'll figure it out every time."

Johnny and Camila eventually won *Battle of the Exes*, and then he was on a roll. He finished in second place on *Rivals II* with Frank Fox (formerly Sweeney) and went on to get his first solo win on *Free Agents*. "That shut a lot of people up, because until that point, one of the big knocks on me was I couldn't win on my own—I needed an alliance, I needed partners, whatever," he says. "I always knew I had the ability to do it, but there's a lot of people out there who questioned it. And I went against this mega-alliance of C.T., Zach [Nichols], and Jordan [Wiseley], and I basically had to go through all of them to win. I kind of forgot everything that I learned about politicking, because I went in and rubbed a lot of people the wrong way right out the gate and put a target on my back. But what stood out to me with that one was that I had the ability to fight my way to the top with my back against the wall since day one, and that was good to know for future seasons because every season after this point, it was like, 'This guy's won enough.'"

After that fifth win, Johnny knew he'd have more enemies than allies. But when his friend Sarah Rice threw him into the last elimination before the final on *Battle of the Exes II*, which he lost with his partner Nany González, he felt like he had no allies left at all. He claims that moment was the most betrayed he'd ever felt in the game. But it turned out to be a blessing in disguise, as it led to him winning his sixth season with Sarah as his partner on *Rivals III*. By the end of that final, Johnny had earned more points than Sarah, so he was given a choice to split the prize money with her . . . or take it all for himself. Citing Sarah's betrayal from the season prior, Johnny declared he was going to "take the money and run," leaving Sarah—and viewers—in absolute disbelief. "I knew it was going to be a big moment, but I didn't know that it was going to be as big of a moment as it ended up being," Johnny says. "It's still, to this day, talked about as the biggest moment ever."

Ever since Johnny had made his debut on *The Challenge*, that had always been his ultimate goal: to make his mark on the franchise. "If you look at all the top, most talked-about *Challenge* moments, whether it's the Backpack or stealing from Sarah or Jordan flipping all the cards and sending himself in against me or who has the most *Challenge* wins, I'm woven into every single one of those story lines," he says. When T.J. gave him the option to steal Sarah's half of the prize money, he knew he couldn't pass up the perfect opportunity to make history again. The move earned him the reputation as *The Challenge*'s biggest villain, but he's never regretted making it. "I like to call myself an embedded producer because I don't approach the show the way most cast members do. I look at it like, what's going to make the best TV? I remember the night before, I was lying there in the tent thinking, 'Fuck, I'm ahead. I'm probably going to win. How am I going to justify doing this? Production obviously wants to either see her do it to me or they want me to do it to her.' I knew it was a massive moment, and if I split the money, we would not be talking about it today. I had to do it."

For his next six seasons after *Rivals III* (*Invasion of the Champions*, *XXX: Dirty 30*, *Vendettas*, *Final Reckoning*, *War of the Worlds*, and *War of the Worlds 2*), Johnny failed to make it to a single final—either he made it all the way until the end and got eliminated right before the final, or he was sent packing at the beginning of the season. But he just couldn't seem to get to the end again. Fans and other players began to speculate that he was now cursed, that stealing the money from Sarah doomed him to never winning another season. "Just so you know, I never believed in this curse," he says. "I think if anything, the only curse that I had was the curse of being too successful. Now, from the second I walked into the house, I had to clock in. From day one, guys like Wes [Bergmann] and C.T., it was like, 'How do we get rid of Bananas?' Now I was facing a lot more adversity and my job got a lot more difficult. Alliances were created simply for the fact of going against me."

It took him a lot longer than it had at the beginning of his *Challenge* career to figure out how to adapt to overcome this particular obstacle. But when Johnny was getting ready to return for *Total Madness*, he realized how he could finally fix the issue. Instead of continuing to fight *against* his biggest enemy, Wes, he needed to do the impossible and work *with* Wes. He reached out to Wes before the season began filming to offer an olive branch, and thus, one of the most unexpected alliances was born. "One of my biggest regrets on *The Challenge* is not putting my bullshit aside with Wes earlier," Johnny says. "When I think back on how much more difficult it made both of our lives and how much more success both of us potentially could have had, had we not continued that on . . . I don't know. But the way that our rivalry ended and our alliance began that season and the way that he went out, it was just such a good story line." Johnny and Wes worked together until they ended up going against each other in an elimination. Johnny beat Wes and eventually won *Total Madness*, getting his seventh win. "Curses be damned! Proving to people that this curse doesn't exist, proving to myself because, I'm not going to lie, that was obviously in the back of my head, 'Is there really a curse?' Finally putting all that to bed was big."

While Johnny hasn't returned in the years since winning *Total Madness*, he's still as involved as ever in the *Challenge* world. He launched his *Death, Taxes, and Bananas* podcast in 2021, where he recaps new episodes and interviews current and past competitors about their time on the show. Plus, he promises he's not done competing on *The Challenge* just yet. "Listen, I could win ten more *Challenge*s and still want to keep showing up and doing something new and different," he says. "I think stepping away from the show for the past few seasons has been good for not just my own personal growth and well-being but also for my stake back on the show. I feel like a lot of the vitriol and hate that had come my way in the past and a lot of the rivalries that I had created have faded out. I mean, I did fifteen seasons in a row, which is psychotic. I needed a chance to rest. I think I'll return refreshed. I also might go back and feel like a total fish out of water, so who knows. It's exciting and terrifying, but I will make my return."

In the meantime, he's focusing on his new career as a TV host for shows like *1st Look* and *Celebrity Sleepover*, where he's finally been able to shed the "character" he's been playing the past fifteen years. "On *The Challenge*, vulnerability is a weakness because you're in a shark tank, and that's why I created this 'Johnny Bananas' persona," he says. "He's larger-than-life and sarcastic and in-your-face and tongue-in-cheek and doesn't take anything seriously, and it was a way to protect myself over the years, like a coat of armor. I owe *The Challenge* everything, but right now I'm enjoying being able to be a more well-rounded, honest version of myself and being comfortable being that person. Maybe on my next season of *The Challenge*, you might see a more warm, kindhearted version of myself—stranger things have happened, and reality is stranger than fiction." Say hello to the next stage of the evolution of Johnny Bananas.

As for the next stage of the evolution of *The Challenge*? We'll just have to wait and see how that unfolds. And if the past two and a half decades are any indication, there's no telling where this franchise—and these champs—will go next.

ACKNOWLEDGMENTS

There are so many people I want to thank who helped make my dream of writing this book a reality. First of all, none of this would have happened without my incredible literary agent, Jon Michael Darga from Aevitas Creative Management. Who would have thought that in less than a year, we'd go from an innocuous email exchange to literally holding this book in our hands?! I'm still in shock. We did it! I never would have taken this massive step forward in my writing career without your being the catalyst for it, so thank you, thank you, thank you. Of course, this book also wouldn't exist without Christian Trimmer, the editorial director at MTV Books, who not only championed the idea for it but also worked with me every step of the way to ensure it was the best it could possibly be. As a longtime fan of *The Challenge*, let alone the author of this book, I can't thank you enough for the care and passion you brought to editing every chapter—and for the kind yet firm pressure I needed to give procrastination a kick in the pants.

All the interviews I did for this book are thanks to Imani Cruz from the Talent and Series Development Department at MTV Networks. Coordinating that schedule was, and I cannot stress this enough, *not* an easy feat. You're an absolute rock star.

Thank you to *Challenge* champs Johnny "Bananas" Devenanzio, Tyler Duckworth, Landon Lueck, Mark Long, Cara Maria Sorbello, Jodi Weatherton, Emily Schromm, Derrick Kosinski, Rachel Robinson, Veronica Portillo, Jordan Wiseley, Hunter Barfield, Yes Duffy, Jonna Mannion, Cynthia Roberts, Alton Williams, Julie Rogers, Syrus Yarbrough, M.J. Garrett, and Darrell Taylor for being open, honest, and vulnerable in their interviews and for taking the time to participate in this book. I know I enjoyed talking with all of you about your experiences, and I hope the fans enjoy reading about them, too. And I also want to give a massive shout-out to everyone on the MTV/Paramount+/ViacomCBS publicity teams I've worked with over the years while writing about *The Challenge*—thank you to Charli Wood, Rebecca Lawlor, Cierra Wiseman, Julie Holland, Nicole Platt, and Brian Bahr for granting me the access I needed to cover the show for *Entertainment Weekly*. Without all those weekly emails and phone calls, setting up interviews and sharing episodes in advance, the opportunity to write this book truly never would have happened. And of course, to my love Kyle Pleva, this whole journey began with you on that fateful day at that aftershow taping (you know the one). I'm so proud of how far we've both come since that day. I cannot accurately put into words how thankful I am for you.

Next, I want to thank my friends and fellow *Challenge* fans for being the best cheerleaders I could have asked for as I worked on this book and for all the years I've written about the show before that. From my *Challenge* fantasy league—Johnny Langan, Will Laws, and Ryan Romania—to the people I immediately text whenever we need to discuss *Challenge* tea—Anthony Lombardo, Sam Highfill, Carolyn Murdock, and Kyle Emory—I love nerding out with all of you. Thanks to my former coworker/now lifelong friend Chance Agard for always being a phone call away when I need to talk through a specific word choice. Thank you to my friend Dan Macalalag for giving me the motivation I needed to finish this book when I got hit with COVID right before the final deadline—you're my hero, for real. And to the best roommate/friend, Rachel Field, thank you for celebrating me and this milestone at every step of the way. I know you already have the perfect bottle of wine ready to be uncorked for when this book is released. To the rest of my friends who supported me on this journey, I love you all for too many reasons to list here.

I want to say a big thank-you to my family, especially my mom and dad, for believing in my potential as an author long before I did. I always wanted to write a book but never thought I'd have the time or even the skills to actually make it happen. You always knew I could, and here we are!

Lastly, thank you to all the fans of *The Challenge* who have read and supported my writing about the show through the years, including this book. Even if you don't agree with my opinions or analysis, that's totally okay! I've thoroughly enjoyed debating all of it with you, and I welcome all your criticism, too. I love this show, and I'm always here to talk about it. Come find me on social media and tell me who you think the *Challenge* GOAT is. I know who I think it is—let's see if you agree.

ABOUT THE AUTHOR

Sydney Bucksbaum is a writer and editor at *Entertainment Weekly*, where she passionately covers all things pop culture—but TV is her one true love. As a longtime fan of *The Challenge*, she gives fans a deeper dive into the world of MTV's long-running competition series past what is shown on TV through her weekly interviews with fan-favorite champs, underdogs, producers, and even host T.J. Lavin himself, as well as writing detailed recaps of episodes with expert analysis. Her work has previously been featured in *Teen Vogue*, *The Hollywood Reporter*, DCComics.com, Mashable, IGN, *Bustle*, *Inverse*, and more. She graduated from Northwestern University's Medill School of Journalism in 2012 and immediately traded the freezing tundra of Chicago for her current home of sunny Los Angeles. In addition to her writing/editing at *EW*, she also cohosts SiriusXM's *Superhero Insider* radio show and is a member of the Television Critics Association and the Hollywood Critics Association.